Roy Court was born in Scotland. After studying chemistry and mathematics in university, he went to work for associated British Maltsters in 1960, carrying out research work into malting and whiskey production. In 1963, he was appointed chief chemist for William Grant & Sons.

In 1965, he moved to Ireland to work for John Jameson & Son as a development distiller. The company merged to form Irish Distillers, and Roy filled a number of senior management roles.

In 1982, he left Irish Distillers to set up a consultancy business in the west of Ireland.

From then until the present, he has worked for a number of companies in the production of whiskey and other products and new product development.

Roy Court

How We Put an 'e' in Whiskey

AUSTIN MACAULEY PUBLISHERS™

LONDON • CAMBRIDGE • NEW YORK • SHARJAH

A CIP catalogue record for this title is available from the British Library.

ISBN 9781528998383 (Paperback)
ISBN 9781528999205 (Hardback)
ISBN 9781528999212 (ePub e-book)

www.austinmacauley.com

First Published (2021)
Austin Macauley Publishers Ltd
25 Canada Square
Canary Wharf
London
E14 5LQ

I wish to acknowledge the help, support and encouragement given to me by Noreen, our son Andrew and our daughter Ruth. Ruth has an honours BSc degree and a postgraduate diploma in brewing and distilling.

Also, the late Dr Pearse Lyons, Professor Inge Russell, David Pym, Aidan O'Sullivan, Jamie Cawley, Susan McGrady, Donal Heavey, Kate McMahon, Ethel Balfe and Mary Berg.

Contents

Foreword

This book is written based on my long experience in the whiskey industry, both in Scotland and finally in Ireland with John Jameson and is not a coffee table book, nor is it a technical manual. I have written this book, which describes the origins of whiskey and its usage, which I hope will interest both technical and non-technical people who have an interest in whiskey. I believe that non-technical people can skip over the technical parts and still find the rest interesting.

Much of what happened in the development of whiskey occurred in the distant past when nothing was written down, and I have used my knowledge of the process to attempt to deduce what actually happened in those days. If in the future, some facts emerge which prove my deductions to be wrong, I hope I will be forgiven.

During the last century, whisky export markets have been dominated by Scotch Whisky, but in more recent times Irish Whiskey has begun to grow significantly on export markets. This means whiskey without an 'e' was considered the only spelling. Now with the development of Irish whiskey, the spelling can be either.

In this book I describe in detail how we gradually developed whiskey spelled with an 'e', so that it now has a growing place on world markets.

Chapter 1
An International Spirit

Whiskey (Whisky) is an amber-coloured alcoholic drink known and enjoyed worldwide. Most whiskeys are preceded by the name of the country of origin, such as 'Scotch whisky', and 'Irish whiskey'. The largest producer of whiskey is the United States, most of which is consumed in its own large domestic market. It is generally agreed that the first whiskey was distilled in Ireland, but with a population of between four, and at the most almost eight million, no viable industry could be sustained without the development of an export market. This came about during the eighteenth century when Irish whiskey was first introduced to England, partly displacing brandy which was the only other spirit then, and for all in the nineteenth century, Irish whiskey dominated the whiskey market in England and the imported market in the United States. This situation continued until the beginning of the twentieth century when, for reasons we will discuss later, Scotch whisky took the lead and has been the majority whisky import worldwide ever since. This, however, is not the end of the game because Irish whiskey exports are currently growing at a much faster rate than

Scotch, and whilst no one knows how it will all end up, the projections for Irish whiskey look very promising.

Whiskey is a self-flavoured product which means that the flavour is derived exclusively from the raw materials and the production process. Brandy, rum, calvados and a whole range of fruit brandies also fall into that category, as does vodka. As such, these products differ from gin and other products which are flavoured.

Irish whiskey is produced mainly from indigenously grown barley and as such it converts a product from Irish farms into a high value export. Most agricultural products have a limited shelf life, but whiskey has a long shelf life and can be exported worldwide.

The word 'whiskey' or 'whisky' is an Anglicisation of the phrase, *Uisce beatha*, Irish for water of life – *eau de vie* in French or *Aquavit* in Danish. In Scotland they call it Whisky and in Ireland, Whiskey. There is no rational explanation as to why this should be so, but as someone who has spent half of his life in Scotland and the other half in Ireland, I believe this reflects the way the Scots and the Irish pronounce the word whiskey.

In practically every international hotel and other up-market outlets worldwide, Scotch whisky and, to a lesser extent, Irish and North American whiskeys are available, sometimes at a very high price. Whiskey is considered to be a very up-market and prestigious drink and this is confirmed by references in books, films and plays, often to specific brands. It is also the international phonetic for the letter 'W'.

Most countries have indigenous alcoholic drinks which are generally consumed by the locals and are usually much cheaper than whiskey, but they lack the complexity, flavour balance and sophistication of whiskey, and to the uninitiated, they often taste quite unpleasant and are consumed more for their effect rather than flavour quality. It is not unusual for regular consumers of the local drink to change over to drinking whiskey when their economic circumstances permit. Many others cannot afford this change.

Scotland is slightly to the north of Ireland and obviously the shortest way from Scotland to the new world takes you to Canada whereas from Ireland you reach the United States and it is interesting to note that in Canada, like Scotland, whiskey is spelt without an 'e' whereas in the United States, like Ireland, Whiskey is spelt with an 'e'.

From its first distillation, believed to have been somewhere in Ireland, whiskey distillation spread throughout the country and onwards to Scotland and beyond. The art was not confined to whiskey because in the south of England and Northern Europe, alcohol produced by distillation was later flavoured with juniper and other botanicals to produce gin.

In general, those who learned how to distil, did so for themselves and their friends, but in the big house, the cook, whose job it was to brew the beer, also became the distiller and provided the occupants of the big house, together with their guests, with this new spirit. Likewise, innkeepers and owners of hotels and taverns distilled and sold the product to their guests. Anyone who has tasted newly distilled whiskey knows that it has a somewhat harsh taste, which is later smoothed out during the maturation period, and for this reason, before maturation was known about, people began to add various ingredients to improve the flavour, such as saffron, sugar, cloves, cinnamon and liquorice. At this stage, its superb qualities led it to be called the 'water of life' which was shortened to 'water' or in Irish, '*Uisce*', later anglicised to 'Whiskey'.

According to current E.C. regulations, whisky or whiskey is described as a spirit drink produced by the distillation of a mash of cereals.

- saccharified by the diastase of the malt contained therein, with or without other natural enzymes.
- fermented by the action of yeast
- distilled at less than 94.8% vol. so that the distillate has an aroma and taste derived from the raw materials used, and matured for at least three years in wooden casks not exceeding 700 litres capacity.

If the above takes place exclusively in Scotland, the whisky can be described as Scotch Whisky, and if it takes place on the island of Ireland, it can be described as Irish Whiskey (please note the Island of Ireland includes Northern Ireland and whiskey can be distilled on one part of the island and matured on the other).

Whiskey which has been distilled and matured on the island of Ireland, using a Scotch Whisky process can, as per the above, be designated Irish Whiskey, but unless there is a taste difference from Scotch Whisky, it is questionable as to whether or not the product would have much credibility on export markets and as such its sales potential could be very limited.

Chapter 2
Drinking Whiskey

If I am asked, I would say that whiskey should be drunk with water, just sufficiently added to eliminate the alcohol burn, but without ice, so that the complexity of all the different flavours can be enjoyed. It is not a drink to be rushed, but to be savoured, slowly, preferably in good company. However, I would also say that you should drink whiskey in whatever manner you enjoy it best, even if that is in a way or in a mix that would not work for me. But I am talking present times, unlike the past. For example, when whiskey was first distilled, there was no central heating or warm cars. People walked or rode on horseback or in some kind of trap, and all this happened in Ireland and Scotland, where in the winter the weather was dark, cold, wet and windy or worse. In these times, whiskey warmed the body and raised the spirits. I once travelled to the Scottish Highlands with a colleague who was born and brought up in London. It was October and there was snow on the mountains and a cold east wind. Having experienced this for a day or so, he said to me that he now understood why in Scotland, porridge and whiskey were essentials.

The famous Scottish entertainer, Sir Harry Lauder, sang the following song.

Just a wee deoch-an-doris, Just a wee yin, that's a'. Just a wee deoch-an-doris, before we gang awa'. There's a wee wifie waitin', In a wee but-an-ben; If you can say, "It's a braw bricht moonlicht nicht."

Ye're a' richt, ye ken.

Roughly translated it means *A deoch-an-doris* is a drink at the door offered before the friend sets off home to his little cottage where his wife is waiting. The Whiskey intended to warm him and raise his spirits for the journey home. The adverse effects of overindulging were well recognised then because the man was asked to say an old Scottish tongue twister to demonstrate that he was fit to travel home.

It is common practice when people are about to drink that they would tip glasses and toast one another. This practice arrives from former times when being offered a drink, it would be normal, first of all, to pass your glass to your host for him to taste so as to ensure that neither he nor his staff were trying to poison you. Gradually, people began to trust their hosts and the glasses were tipped simply to say, "I trust you and I don't need you to taste my drink."

Americans often ask for a whiskey on the rocks. I think this largely refers to the ambience, where it is either hot or cold outside; indoors is usually well heated and ice melts quickly and serves both to cool and dilute the drink. In central Scotland it was common to hear people ask for a 'half and a half'. That was a half measure of whiskey and a half pint of beer. The whiskey was thrown back straight (something I do not approve of) and then the beer was drunk slowly. They used to say that the whisky lit a fire which was then slowly quenched with the beer. Much depended on the whisky type. In central Scotland it was mainly blended whisky, whereas in the Highlands and in Ireland, Scottish malt whisky and Irish Pot Still Whiskey, being much more flavoursome products, were more usually taken slowly with water.

The addition of water and ice to whiskey merely serves to reduce the alcohol content and to cool the drink. People have different sensitivities to alcohol bite and burn and adding the right amount of water optimises the taste characteristics. A friend of mine, when asked how he would like his whiskey, used to say, "I drink it half and half and put in plenty of water."

Sometimes whiskey is mixed with other things, which has the effect of changing the flavour and this way the possibilities are enormous. Such a drink may have a different taste altogether and would be a drink in its own right rather than a whiskey. This is what we call a cocktail. In the United States the concept of cocktails evolved. One story as to the origin of cocktails is attributed to King Axlotl VIII of Mexico at around the year 1800, when he had a meeting with an American General of the Southern States. At one point the King ordered refreshments and a beautiful woman brought 'a strange assortment of her own brewing'. In these times people had a fear of being poisoned and did not want to be first to taste any drink. Usually the host would be asked to taste the drink first, but there was an embarrassment in asking this of the King. The woman, who immediately understood the situation, tasted it herself, thus all embarrassment was avoided. When the meeting eventually came to a satisfactory conclusion, the general asked if he might know the name of the lady. The King, who had never before seen her, said proudly, "That is my daughter, Coctel." On leaving the meeting, the General vowed to ensure that her name would be honoured all over America.

The idea of mixing drinks gradually spread through the United States, where the name was anglicised to 'Cocktail', and eventually to the rest of the world. Cocktails need not necessarily be based on whiskey; any spirit can be used. One famous gin described itself as 'The heart of a good cocktail'. In 1930, the Savoy Hotel in London issued its first cocktail book.

Most spirits have an alcoholic strength of about 40% by volume (80 U.S. Proof). At that strength there is a lot of alcohol burn in the mouth and most people prefer to reduce the 'heat' by adding ice and other ingredients, which not only reduces the alcohol burn but can give the drink a wide range of strengths, flavours, and colours, so that each cocktail has its individual character. There are five basic features to a successful cocktail – start with your chosen spirit and add something sweet like a liqueur or cordial, followed by water, soda, or juice to dilute the alcohol. Then add ice and garnish.

Cocktails really came into their own during prohibition, because if you were seen holding a glass apparently full of fruit juice, who could say that there was not a measure of illicit liquor in there? Also, in the United States there is a puritanical element in which people do not ask for a neat spirit but instead ask for a spirit with the tiniest addition of something which would allow them to call it a cocktail. I remember being in Baltimore, Maryland, many years ago in a restaurant where the speciality of the house was a very dry martini. The barman put gin and ice into a cocktail glass. Then he sprayed dry vermouth from an atomiser to form a cloud, the glass was then passed through the vermouth cloud. It was a great success even though people were effectively drinking neat gin.

Some barmen are famous for their cocktails and some drinks like Southern Comfort have their origins as famous cocktails. I have watched barmen skilfully throwing small amounts of this and that with ice, either into a jug, or cocktail shaker. The contents were then poured into two chilled glasses and came exactly to the rim to make excellent cocktails. There are scores of books with cocktail recipes and I do not propose to repeat them here, save to tell you about my favourite cocktail. It is a well-known traditional cocktail called a 'Manhattan'.

To make a perfect Manhattan, you start with Kentucky Bourbon and mix it one third each with Italian vermouth – the red stuff. Then extra dry French vermouth, which is the white stuff, (but not Bianco). Stir these in a glass after adding one drop of Angostura Bitters, then pour into two cocktail glasses containing ice and finally garnish with one or two maraschino cherries. This gives a perfect Manhattan cocktail for two.

Chapter 3
The Four Miracles
That Gave Us Whiskey

I describe a miracle as something good that happens, but how it happens is not understood. All four miracles that gave us whiskey were not understood when they happened and so were true miracles then. Today most, but not all, have been explained, though some mysteries still remain.

The first miracle was the advent of malt. This happened many thousands of years ago and it probably happened by accident. Who could have imagined that barley, rye, or some other cereal, which had been allowed to grow, ever so slightly and then dried could look almost exactly like the original cereal, but to have undergone very significant changes. The change from cereal into malt enables it to be brewed with hot water or to supply the necessary enzymes to convert the starches of other cereals into fermentable liquid called wort.

Freshly baked bread showing how the expanding carbon dioxide from the fermentation stretches the fibres of the dough to create a soft texture

Nothing was known about fermentation, or indeed about the existence of yeast. All that was known was that when flour was mixed with water to make dough, a miracle occurred which caused the dough to rise so that when it was baked, it had the open light texture we all associate with bread. For this reason some cultures regard bread as sacred, and as such it is not cut with a knife but always broken. In Biblical times when at the Passover, the Israelites are reported to have eaten unleavened bread, this would not have been reported as such, unless it was normal for them to have leavened bread, made from dough which had been allowed to rise. Under the right conditions, yeast, in the presence of sugars, produces a mixture of carbon dioxide and alcohol. In breadmaking the alcohol disappears during baking in the oven and the carbon dioxide causes the dough to rise. When wort made from malt was allowed to stand, bubbles of carbon dioxide were seen to emerge, and the wort gradually, over a few days, acquired an alcoholic taste. This was all to do with the presence of yeast which was unknown in the early days.

Bloom on black grapes

Yeast is one of nature's miracle products, because when a plant grows, and that is a wonderful thing in itself, what is even more wonderful is that the plant eventually dies and rots away. Imagine what the planet would be like if this did not happen. There is a whole army of different bacteria to assist in the decay of plant material, but plants also contain sugars, the source of energy from the sun which fuels their growth. These are large and complex molecules which need special treatment to reduce them progressively into smaller molecules as part of the decaying process. For this purpose, nature invented yeast. It appears on all kinds of plants – most notably as the bloom on grapes. Nowadays, yeasts of many types including distillers' yeast are produced industrially for sale.

In the areas around the Mediterranean, grapes grow in abundance. If grapes are placed in a large tank, the bloom on their skins will gradually convert the sugars present into alcohol, so that after several months, the liquid is poured off leaving the solids behind; the liquid will be red wine. In the past, the presence of yeast and the part it played were unknown. Instead, the wine was regarded as sacred and as such, it was used in religious services, a practice which still exists today. Wine was being produced for many centuries BCE as evidenced by its presence in the tomb of King Tutankhamen in 1344 BCE. All the wine referred to here is red wine; white wine requires technology and appeared much later.

Early mariners knew that if a sponge was held in the steam from boiling sea water, the water squeezed from the sponge was 'sweet'. That is the salt from the sea water was left behind and the condensed steam was pure water. This is distillation. Much later, the concept was used to extract fragrances from plants in the manufacture of perfumes. It was probably around the tenth century when alcohol was first distilled and described as water that burned. First it was used for medicinal purposes, and later it is believed, first of all in Ireland, to convert beer made from malt into whiskey – a miracle of monumental proportions.

Beer is mainly water, which we could call the primary constituent. The secondary constituent would be alcohol and then there are a large number of tertiary constituents. When this is distilled at least twice in a copper pot, some of the water, all of the alcohol and a selection of tertiary constituents are collected as new whiskey. The remainder is disposed of as waste. The way a simple copper pot, in the hands of a skilled distiller, can select the wanted parts like alcohol, and then select the most desirable of the tertiary substances, was at that time truly a miracle and even today some of the detail is not fully understood.

Whiskey was originally consumed as soon as it was distilled, but it was later found to improve when stored in wooden casks, usually made of oak. Maturation in wooden casks is such an important part of whiskey-making, that a minimum number of years for this is now enshrined in law. Even today, what happens during maturation is not fully understood. During maturation the whiskey acquires a beautiful golden/amber colour and undergoes changes in flavour smoothness and balance – a true miracle.

When next you sit down to enjoy a glass or two of whiskey, hopefully in the company of a good friend, think back over the thousands of years during which the confluence of these four miracles has given whiskey the tradition, complexity and excellence for which it is known today.

Chapter 4
Malt

Malt is cereal, usually barley, which has been steeped in water for about two days until the moisture content reaches about 44% and allowed to grow for about five days. Growth is then stopped by drying on a kiln. The rootlets are removed by gentle screening and the final malt looks almost the same as the original cereal. The two can easily be told apart by biting a corn. Malt has a friable biscuit texture, whereas barley is hard and tough to bite. During the malting process the cereal undergoes a number of changes which enable it to be brewed with hot water or to supply the necessary enzymes to convert the starches of other cereals into fermentable liquid called wort.

It is believed that agriculture, including the growing of barley, began approximately 12,000 years ago, and with it came the necessity to store the crop after harvest for two purposes. First there was a necessity to retain sufficient grain to use as next season's seeding stock, then there was the need for the rest of the harvest to be available throughout the year and this involved storage.

It is assumed that a quantity of barley in storage became wet as a result of rainfall or flooding and began to grow.

When this was discovered, it no doubt brought about a certain amount of panic and the growing barley was probably spread out to dry in the sun. This was the discovery of malt.

The malt was found to be significantly different from the barley that produced it; for example, it was crisp and friable unlike barley which is tough. It was soon found that when malt was ground up and hot water added, it would produce an amber-coloured wort which would ferment naturally to form a simple type of ale. Ways were found to remove the solids to give a drink that was probably quite cloudy, but nevertheless it became a popular beverage throughout the known world. It should be mentioned that the use of hops came very much later.

The sweet, satisfying taste of malt, led to its use in the baking of a whole range of foods, and indeed drinks in the form of ale, and to supply for these uses, malting evolved as a craft.

Malt is made by soaking barley in water in a tank called a 'steep' so that it absorbs water which triggers growth. A maltster will tell you of a 'hand and eye' method to calculate how long to steep the barley. Subtract the Fahrenheit temperature of the steeping water from 100, to get the number of hours, the barley must be steeped. So, if the water is 60°F, the steeping time is 40 hours. It is also necessary to change the water once or twice during the steeping period. The water is then drained off, and in the traditional method the steeped barley is spread thickly on a floor. The growing process generates heat and the temperature of the germinating barley is carefully monitored. The ideal growing temperature is about 18°C, and as the temperature approaches this value, the malt is spread progressively more thinly. It is also turned and ploughed a few times per day, traditionally by hand. The growing period takes about five days during which rootlets develop and the new shoot, called the acrospire, grows up the entire length of the corn, underneath the husk.

An ear of barley

When the acrospire has grown almost the entire length of the barley corn, the malt, at this stage called 'green malt', is ready to be kilned. The traditional malt kiln has a perforated floor with a furnace underneath and a pagoda-like structure above to create the necessary draft. The malt is spread uniformly on the perforated floor and the furnace is lit. The flow of hot air from the furnace passes through the bed of malt, removing the moisture until a final moisture content of between four and six percent is reached. At this point the rootlets are removed and malt can be stored until it is used. Once again great care is exercised in controlling the kilning temperature. Malt used for distilling is kilned at relatively low temperatures and is called pale malt. If higher temperatures are used, the malt acquires colour which can be anything from amber to black and is used to brew beers of equivalent colours. The malt does not normally acquire flavour from the fuel used in the furnace but, for certain distilling malts, the kiln is fired wholly or partly with peat. Whiskeys made from this type of malt have a distinctive and unique flavour derived from the peat, but this is not to everyone's taste. I can find no confirmation to the old rumour that the peating process is enhanced by the sound of bagpipes!

The traditional malting process is very labour intensive and various methods of mechanisation have been derived over the years, up to and including modern times when the entire malting process in some plants is carried out in a single vessel.

Floor malting at Bowmore distillery, Scotland

Now we know how barley is malted, but we don't know why. To look at this we must go back to the basic cereal. Cereals have evolved from wild grasses which have been bred and selected so as to lend themselves to farming, giving reliable harvests of plump corns. The fact that these grasses, and then the domesticated cereal, have survived for many thousands of years, means that each plant has yielded the necessary seed to produce at least one viable plant at the next and subsequent harvests, and so, as with all living things, the ability to reproduce is the first and main objective. In ancient times, the grasses, when ripened, would fall over and the ears would be scattered in the ground. These seeds would have to survive cold and wet winter conditions until spring came along, and then have the necessary supply of energy until they had developed enough rootlet growth and leaves to sustain themselves.

A plant grows by obtaining carbon dioxide from the atmosphere, which with the help of a substance called 'chlorophyll', the green substance in plants, and in the presence of sunlight, combines with water collected by the roots. This forms two main groups of sugars and releases oxygen to the atmosphere in the process. One type of sugar is the starting material for the formation of cellulose from which stems and leaves are produced, and the other, which in cereals is glucose. This sugar is the source of energy for the growing plant; To sustain the early part of growth until the new plant can fend for itself, the cereal lays in a stock of energy, in a form that will survive intact during the cold and wet winter months. To do this the glucose combines with itself to form long chains or polymers. This particular polymer is called starch. To further protect the starch, it is

29

locked up in cells composed of protein. The long-branched chain structure is much tougher than a simple sugar. For example, anyone who has worked with corn flour or other starch material knows that it does not combine with water other than by boiling; unlike simple sugars which dissolve very quickly in water.

When the plant begins to grow, it must release the starch from the protein cells and break the chains down to usable lengths. This is achieved by the development or release of certain enzymes. First of all, the enzyme proteinase attacks the protein cell walls converting the protein into soluble amino-acids and similar substances, which results in the starch becoming accessible. Then along comes alpha-amylase – the dextrinising enzyme which attacks the starch reducing the chain size to give a range of substances called dextrins which are water soluble. Finally, another enzyme system called beta amylase breaks down the dextrins into a sugar called maltose which contains two glucose units joined together. This is used as the energy source for the growing plant.

Malted Barley

The malting process causes the starch to be released and modified and enzymes like the two types of enzymes to be activated, and at this point kilning stops further development. The resultant malt can then, after milling, be brewed with hot water so that the starch is metabolised to form wort, containing fermentable sugars like maltose. This is the objective of the distiller because maltose can be fermented with yeast to give alcohol, the primary constituent, other than water, of whisky. During this fermentation, the reduction of fermentable sugars in the wort make space for further fermentable sugars to be formed. This action contributes up to an additional 20% of the final alcohol yield.

Chapter 5
Brewing

Ever since the malting process was discovered, believed to be almost 12,000 years ago, ale was produced by brewing malt with water. In regions where there was no wine, ale was the only alcoholic drink available and was widely consumed. In the big house, the cook was responsible for brewing the ale and for those who did not live in a big house, inns and hostelries sold ale by the tankard. Over the years the process was gradually improved but no hops were used until much later.

Distillers' requirements differ somewhat from brewers, for example, brewers normally brew at 65^0C but distillers use the slightly lower value of 62.5^0C. This is because distillers wish to preserve some of the malt enzymes which continue working during the fermentation. Brewers, on the other hand, have no interest in preserving the enzymes because the brewer immediately boils the wort prior to fermentation. The type of brewing described here, where the ground malt and water of the appropriate temperature are mixed together so that the desired final temperature of the mash is achieved, is called 'infusion mashing'.

An interior view of a lauter tun showing the perforated false bottom and the rotating knives which can be raised and lowered for gentle raking. They can also be used by changing the angle for removing the spent grains

In this process the ground malt and hot water are mixed to give a final temperature of 144^0F (62^0C). The mixture is gently stirred and allowed to settle. The wort is then drained through the perforated false bottom of the mash tun on which the grains have settled to form a filter. The clear wort obtained in this manner is cooled to about 18^0C and transferred to the wash back (fermentation vessel) where it is mixed with yeast for fermentation. A second water is applied to the grains at a higher temperature and once again drained, cooled and added to the first one in the wash back. A third, very hot, water is applied and drained as before, but not cooled, and returned to the brewing tank to be used in the next mash. There are differences of opinion as to whether the returned third water should be used as the first or second water of the next mash. One particular source I know, believes you should always mash in with fresh water and that the returned third water should be used as the second water of the next mash. This process continues to be used in Scotland for making Malt Whisky, but in Ireland the introduction of mixed cereal brewing called for a different approach. A malt tax, which will be discussed later, was introduced, bringing about the inclusion of unmalted barley in the mash.

Barley is the seed of the plant, and so it is structured to protect the energy source in the form of starch, so that it would survive intact during the winter. For this reason, the starch granules are enclosed in cells with protein walls and as such the starch would not be exposed to the normal malt enzymes. This problem is addressed in two ways – first of all, the barley is very finely ground to break up some of the cells mechanically and expose the starch, and then the mash is given a so called 'protein rest' in which the malt proteinase is allowed to metabolise the remaining protein walls, exposing the starch. Unfortunately, the proteolytic enzymes in malt are heat sensitive, with a thermal death point not much above 50°C. For this reason the mash is originally made at 50° C and allowed to rest for about an hour after which the mash is heated up to normal distillers brewing temperature of 62.5°C. To do this was problematic because the mash tuns then were made of cast iron which there was no way of heating, and so the heating must be done externally. After a mash had been completed and the wort drained through the bed of grains at the bottom, it was normal in Irish distilleries also to side-let, which resulted in a fair amount of particulate matter in the wort. The wort was then cooled and sent to a wash back for fermentation. In the meantime, a number of after-mashings took place at increasing temperatures and the resultant wort returned to the coppers to be combined in an elaborate order. Coppers were used because presumably they would have been heated originally by a furnace, but this was later changed to internal steam heating. Copper is exceptionally toxic to malt enzymes and for this reason the coppers were internally tinned.

This process is called decoction brewing and it is interesting to note that it is widely used in central Europe, particularly Germany, for lager production. This is not because they used unmalted barley, because it is prohibited by the German 'purity law' which permits beer to be made only from four ingredients: water, malt, hops and yeast. In the traditional German process, after the initial mashing at 50°C, some of the wort is removed and heated up in, what the Germans call, a kettle. This is returned to the mash, progressively increasing the temperature until the brewers' temperature of 65°C is reached. Today, in Germany it is normal to use a mash kettle with heating panels to carry out the protein rest, and then progressively increase the heat after which the mash is transferred to the lauter tun where the wort is drained off (lauter being the German word for filter). A lauter tun is a modern type of mash tun and is now being widely used in the Scottish and Irish whiskey distilleries. The use of this type of brewing in Europe is based on the fact that European barleys are higher in protein content than those of Britain and of Ireland. Proteins are difficult substances to deal with and are liable to cause haze in the final product; this is obviously unsatisfactory in a lager and so the vast majority of the malt proteins are metabolised in the brewing process, thus avoiding the problem.

A lauter tun

Having managed to brew and ferment successfully using this process, it was found that distilling in the normal two-stage pot still process did not give satisfactory results and so a three-stage process was developed which was much more complex and which produced the final distillate at 86% ABV.

Chapter 6
Fermentation

Scientists have recently discovered that about ten million years ago, due to a mutation, early man and some apes acquired the ability to metabolise ethanol, the alcohol we drink today in wine, beer and spirits. The only source of alcohol they would have had was in overripe fruit which had begun to ferment. It was not in their interest to become in any way intoxicated because life was too dangerous then and any loss of control could be fatal. It seems, therefore, that overripe fermenting fruit was a last resort when better quality and more nutritious fruit was not available.

Many centuries later when life was more stable and consequently safer, it was discovered that grapes, which grew in abundance in the area around the Mediterranean, were placed in a large vessel and allowed to stand for some months, the liquid which could be poured off was red wine. There can be little doubt that they drank this for pleasure and were aware of the alcoholic effects it produced. Red wine is therefore the simplest kind of wine to make, but eventually they discovered that if the grapes were first pressed and only the juice fermented, white wine would result. Red wine is made from grapes and white wine is made from grape juice.

All this had happened, long before the death of Egyptian Pharaoh King, Tut An Khamun, in 1344 BCE, because in his tomb, when it was opened by Egyptologist Howard Carter in 1925, there were jars of wine bearing the name of the vineyard in which they were produced. The wine, of course, had all evaporated. This means that for many thousands of generations, people who lived in the Mediterranean region had access to alcohol and who were used to drinking regularly and avoiding some of the more extreme effects of alcohol. This can be contrasted with our experience of people who had no such exposure. Northern Europeans, including Celts and Eskimos, also Red Indians and Aborigines, all of whom discovered alcohol recently and many were unable to cope with it. Perhaps this is a clue as to the origins of alcoholism among certain individuals.

If there could be anything more wonderful than watching a plant grow, sometimes from the tiniest seed to perhaps a huge tree, it is the fact that when the plant dies, it rots down to return to the simple ingredients from which it was made. Plants grow when sunlight reacts with chlorophyll, (the green stuff in the leaves) which catalyses the reaction of carbon dioxide from the atmosphere with water and other nutrients collected by the roots, to form two main types of sugars, one to build the structure of the plant as stems and leaves and the other to provide a source of energy. When the plant dies, this process has to be reversed and for this purpose nature has developed yeast. Yeast can be seen as the bloom on grapes and in various forms is widely available in the atmosphere. Yeast reacts with the very complex structure of sugars to convert them into carbon dioxide and alcohol – much simpler substances. It causes the fermentation of grapes to produce wine, where the carbon dioxide bubbles off into the atmosphere and the remaining liquid becomes alcoholic. Equally, when mixed with dough in bread making, the carbon dioxide causes the bread to rise, stretching the proteins of the flour and creating the open texture of bread.

Of course, the ancients knew nothing of this and the fact that grapes fermented and bread was 'leavened', was assumed to be a result of magical qualities and as such both bread and wine were regarded as sacred and often used in religious ceremonies; even today in some cultures, bread, because of its so-called sacred qualities, is never cut with a knife, but broken apart with the hands. One wonders what these cultures would make of our sliced pan?

Today, yeast is produced in yeast factories, which supply it to bakers, brewers and distillers, either as liquid yeast, pressed into cakes, or dried, according to what is appropriate to each industry. Yeast is produced by aerobic fermentation as opposed to alcohol which is produced by anaerobic fermentation. The former requires vast amounts of air to be blown into the fermentation vessel, otherwise quantities of alcohol will also be formed. The final yeast was traditionally pressed into cakes with a moisture content of approximately 34% and this was used in the fermentation at the rate of 2% of the weight of the original cereal. Dried yeast is also available which has a moisture content of about 8.2%, and if this is to be used the addition rate has to be adjusted accordingly based on the calculated dry weight. Dried yeast has to be slowly hydrated before it can be used. Pressed yeast has a maximum shelf life under refrigeration of about two weeks, after which its viability falls off rapidly, whereas dried yeast can be effectively stored under refrigeration for up to one year. In more recent times, the Scottish distillers have availed of liquid yeast which is delivered by tanker for more or less immediate use.

The wort produced by brewing is placed in the fermenting vessel, or wash back as it is called in the distilling industry, and yeast is added. If cake yeast is to be used, it is very often broken into pieces and spread over the bottom of the wash back, in which case great care has to be taken cooling the wort so that an initial quantity of hot wort does not go into the wash back and damage the yeast.

Unlike brewing, where the wort is boiled and therefore sterile, the distiller's wort is not sterile and this results in two effects; first of all the malt enzymes remain active during fermentation, particularly so once the level of fermentable sugars begins to reduce producing additional fermentable materials. Experimental work has shown that up to 20% of the final alcohol yield is attributable to this. The second point is that bacteria, which arrive via the raw material and from the ambience, produce acids which gradually lower the pH of the fermentation. A healthy fermentation begins at a pH of about 5.6 and ends with a pH of about four. If the final pH is much lesser than four, it indicates an infection in the system and the cleaning regime should be checked out.

Traditionally, whiskey distilleries evolved where there was a well-established dairy industry; this would include Scotland, Ireland, Canada, Kentucky and Tennessee. The reason for this is that where milk is widely produced and used, quantities will be spilled or allowed to go sour. Nature's way of eliminating these things includes the bacterium *lactobacillus* which breaks down the main sugar in milk called lactose into lactic acid. Lactic acid has a particularly bitter and unpleasant taste. However, it is virtually non-volatile and is eliminated in the distillation process. Another organism called *aceto bacillus* produces acetic acid which is volatile but does not have an unduly unpleasant taste. The production of these two acids contribute towards the gradual lowering of the pH during fermentation and facilitates the formation of esters. Esters are pleasant-tasting organic substances which exist in many fruits and contribute widely towards the final pleasant flavour. For example, the ester *ethyl two-trans-four-cis-decadienoate* is largely responsible for the taste of pears Where the alcohol content of the fermentation is low, acids and alcohols combine to form a range of different esters but under these conditions the reaction is reversible and so as esters are formed, some revert to their original acid plus alcohol. However, as the alcohol concentration increases, the esters become much more stable. This applies particularly during pot distillation where esters pass into the low wines going from an alcoholic strength of about 8% up to about 20%. This is one mechanism whereby flavour is developed in whiskey manufacture and how lactic esters play an important part.

Japan is a country with what is now a large whiskey manufacturing industry, but unlike the aforementioned countries, they have no tradition of dairy production. For this reason, Japanese whiskeys formerly had their own unique taste which was rather different from whiskey as we know it, and to overcome this problem the Japanese purchased malt whisky from Scotland and from Ireland to blend with their own indigenous product. In more recent times the Japanese have devised a method to introduce laboratory-cultured lactobacillus into their fermentations resulting in an outstanding improvement in the taste characteristics of the final product.

During fermentation heat is evolved, and over the two to three days the fermentation ideally reaches about 30°C. To achieve this, much depends on the starting temperature; I would suggest the ideal to be 18°, but in cold weather there may be a case to increase this up as far as the low 20°s. The size of the wash back, and whether it is made of timber or of stainless steel, and the weather conditions all play a part in this temperature rise but the yeast dies at about 33°C, and so that should be the top temperature permitted. In some distilleries the wash backs are cooled.

The duration of the fermentation depends on a number of factors, particularly on the original gravity. If it is attempted to distil a wash which is less than fully fermented, absolutely uncontrollable froth will result, froth which cannot even be controlled by the addition of proprietary anti-foam agents. As a rough rule of thumb, fermentation requires an equal number of hours as the excess gravity over 1000. A good indication as to when fermentation is complete is the final gravity which should ideally be 998, often described as two under - two degrees less than pure water which is 1000. Fermentations which fail to come below 1000 are suspect; this may be due to defective raw materials, or to the more usual problem in distilleries – infection.

Some fermentations, particularly for 100% malt, are very frothy, in which case the washback is fitted with mechanical switchers to beat down the froth.

Chapter 7
The Magic of Distillation

Whiskey comes about when the magic of distillation is used to refine beer made from cereals. The brewing of cereals to make beer was known back in ancient times, some thousands of years BCE, but distillation was a much more recent discovery. Nevertheless, it all happened so long ago that we cannot be sure of the details. However, it is generally accepted that the invention of the *El Embic,* probably around the fifth century, was the key.

Absolutely no reference to distillation or to spirits has ever been found in the writings of the ancient Greeks or Romans. However, in the third century A.D. it is reported that a process was used by sailors in which sea water was boiled in a vessel with a large sponge suspended above it. Water was later squeezed from the sponge and found to be 'sweet', that is free from salt. This is a simple form of distillation in which the water, the volatile material, passes into the vapour phase by boiling, and is re-formed when this vapour is cooled. The salt and other non-volatile materials are left behind in the boiling vessel.

Anyone who has read about ancient times, or, as I have, visited the ruins of the biblical City of Ephesus, located in what is now Turkey, or Knossos in Crete must have been aware of the casual attitudes that people had to all sorts of waste disposal and indeed to personal hygiene. It must be assumed that, when there was an assembly of any number of people, as in such cities, there would be a demand for something to try to counteract the unpleasant odours which must have existed. The ancients discovered that when certain materials, mainly plants & roots like saffron, jasmine, rose petals, citrus peels and sandalwood etc. were thrown on to a fire, pleasant aromas came through the smoke. Those words in Latin *per fume* gave rise to the English language word 'perfume'. The challenge was how to separate the perfume from the smoke. I know that any whiskey enthusiast will be disappointed, as indeed I was, to discover that distillation was first invented to produce perfume.

In the 10th century, Arab physicians reported the distillation of roses. This appears to be the first reference to the invention of the *el embic*. This was a round pot with a narrow neck and a pipe leading off, through which the vapour was cooled and collected. The vessel was probably originally made with some kind of an earthenware material and heated on a fire to drive the fragrances from the starting material. The neck of the *el embic* appears to have been air-cooled, and so highly volatile materials like alcohol, if indeed any were present in the vapour, would not have been condensed but merely escaped into the atmosphere, whereas less volatile materials, such as those used in perfumery, would have been condensed into a liquid form.

A manuscript entitled *Mappæ Clavicula,* written in the 12th century, describes how strong wine, with salt added, is heated in a suitable vessel and a flammable 'water' is obtained, which when absorbed into a piece of cloth, burns 'without consuming the cloth'. This was clearly 'alcohol' – one of the few Arabic words to find its way into the English language. An earlier copy of this manuscript dated the 10th century carries no mention of this, and so it can be assumed that the distillation of alcohol began between the 10th and 12th centuries. Reports of wine having been distilled came in the 13th century, mainly from France, into what was described as *eau de vie*. This work was undertaken largely in monastic communities because they provided a stable and, indeed, learned environment for processes like this to be developed. This was particularly necessary given the very short life expectation at that time.

Members of the monastic communities were also the physicians of the time and availability of alcohol allowed them to take advantage of its medicinal properties and also as a solvent which they used to extract medicines from plants and herbs. Alcohol was immediately recognised for its medicinal properties and regarded as some sort of a panacea. This is not surprising because even today many drinks are recognised either as aperitifs, to stimulate the appetite, or digestives to settle the stomach. Hot whiskey or 'toddy' are also known as treatment for colds, although some say they simply make the cold more bearable. Brandy with port is often used to settle an upset stomach.

Much of the early distillation took place during the 13th century, in countries around the Mediterranean, where there was a plentiful supply of wine available, from which to distil alcohol. Some of these spirits were called 'burnt wine', which was later anglicised to 'brandy'. There can be no doubt that some brandy was drunk for pleasure but the main use for the alcohol produced then was for medicinal purposes.

The seas and oceans were the highways at that time and monastic communities sprung up along the coasts of the Mediterranean, and later the Atlantic Ocean. This way, they spread as far as Ireland where there are the remains of one large monastic community at a place called Clonmacnoise on the River Shannon. In these days it would have been possible to sail all the way from the Mediterranean and up the River Shannon to that site. Today, it would be more difficult because of the presence of the Ardnacrusha hydroelectric station on the River Shannon.

Knowledge was spread throughout the monastic communities and it seems likely that some came as far as Clonmacnoise. We cannot be sure that it happened there but it does seem to be the most likely place. They had heard about the distillation of alcohol and had probably received some. It is easy to imagine that one day an expert in the art of distillation arrived in Clonmacnoise and was asked to make some alcohol. He would have described how to make a still and the most convenient material available to them for this purpose was copper. So, they had a copper pot closed at the top with a long pipe which was coiled and cooled with a stream of cold water. The next stage was to fill it with wine, but there was no wine, because grapes do not grow easily in Ireland and there was no tradition of wine making. However, there was a long tradition of drinking ale made from malted barley and this was before the days when hops were added, so it was decided to fill the still with beer. The absence of hops was fortunate because the presence of hops would have had a significant negative impact on the product taste. When the early distillate was tasted, it had the clearly identifiable characteristics which we would associate with new whiskey or poitin. This was the piece of magic that gave us whiskey. There were lots of developments yet to come including maturation in wood, but for now the concept of distilling beer into whiskey spread rapidly and was soon regarded as a national pastime.

During the years that followed there was a gradual transition from domestic production to larger scale industrial type of operations. Larger units at that time required a source of motive power of which the only option was water, and so distilleries were sited close to rivers which not only provided them with water for their process and for cooling, but supplied motive power to drive a water wheel which powered the various items of equipment within the plant.

Chapter 8
The Anatomy of a Pot Still

The vast majority of whiskeys produced worldwide depend to some extent on the pot still which makes an important contribution to the flavour and character of the final product. Unlike column stills, pot stills do not fit any well-established set of rules, and for this reason distilling in pot stills has often been referred to as a black art.

A liquid contains moving particles or molecules; the more the liquid is heated, the faster these move, and when they stop moving entirely, the liquid freezes. These molecules move in random directions and some break through the surface like a fish jumping out of the sea but, unlike fish, they don't immediately return to the liquid. This means that any liquid has above it a layer of vapour which causes the vapour pressure. This increases as the temperature increases and when the vapour pressure is equal to atmospheric pressure, the liquid boils.

When you fill an electric kettle with water and have a system whereby you can measure the usage of electricity, if this is constant, the temperature will continue to increase until the kettle comes to the boil. This is the boiling point of the liquid, and if you continue to heat the kettle (provided it's not one that automatically switches off when it comes to the boil), the temperature of the water will remain unchanged and the electrical energy will be used entirely in converting the liquid into vapour. This amount of heat is called the latent heat of vaporisation and is an important factor when discussing stills. The latent heat of vaporisation varies for different liquids; for example, for water 2260 kilojoules per kilogram and for alcohol 837 kilojoules per kilogram. It should be noted that the energy required to distil water is considerably greater than that for distilling alcohol, and with pot still distillation there is always a proportion of water present, and as that distillation proceeds the water content of the distillate increases considerably.

When a mixture of two or more liquids is boiled, the one which is most volatile boils preferentially, and when there are small quantities of other liquids present their volatility is influenced by the proportions of the two main liquids present.

There is a set of rules governing the way in which two liquids distil but this assumes them to be so called ideal liquids. Water and alcohol are far from being ideal liquids. The graph shows the composition of vapour in alcohol water mixtures. It is interesting to note that at about 96% alcohol by volume, the liquid and vapour composition are the same. This is called an azeotrope. Where an azeotrope is formed, the two liquids behave as if they were a single substance and no separation is possible by means of simple distillation.

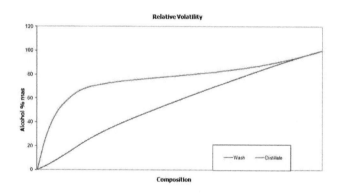

When a mash of malted barley with, or without, other unmalted cereal is fermented, it is usual to have a wash with alcohol content in the order of 8 % by volume. As can be seen from the diagram, the equivalent vapour composition would be about 40% by volume. However, as distillation proceeds, that alcohol content of the wash progressively diminishes; this causes the equilibrium vapour composition to diminish. The process continues until the wash is substantially free from alcohol. The distillation is normally stopped when the alcoholic content of the distillate reaches 1% by volume, which, referring to our diagram, is equivalent to 0.1% alcoholic strength of the content of the pot. We know of no simple mathematical way of making these calculations, however we have designed a computer program which can do this.

We know from experience that if a pot still, filled with wash at about 8% by volume, is distilled, the collected low wines will represent about one third of the volume of the original wash and consequently the low wines will have an alcoholic strength in the order of 24%. This is not strong enough to be whiskey and so a second distillation is necessary. This takes place in the spirit still from which three fractions are taken. The first fraction, called foreshots, represent between 4-5% of the total alcohol in the pot and can be identified by a simple water test. When a quantity of water is added to foreshots, a blue opalescence appears. This can be monitored until a point is reached where there is no longer opalescence and then the new spirit is collected. At most distilleries, rather than making a series of water tests on the foreshots, a time in minutes is arrived at where it is deemed that all of the foreshots have been collected.

The new spirit comes from the middle cut from the spirit still, some call it the heart of the distillation, and distillation continues until the alcoholic strength of the distillate reaches a predetermined point at which the distillate is diverted to the low wines, foreshots and feints receiver and is called feints. Two important points arise. The charge in the spirit still normally consists of all of the low wines plus the recycled foreshots and feints. The volatility of the secondary constituents is highly dependent on the alcoholic strength of the charge in the spirit still, and as it subsequently reduces, this has a fundamental bearing on the character of the resultant spirit. The second point is that the alcohol content of the final spirit must equal the alcohol content introduced into the system by virtue of the low wines less a small amount of distillation loss. Given the limitations of a simple pot still and the regulations imposed by the EC, Excise and Scotch Whisky Association, it is not possible to adjust these values. Consequently the character of the final spirit is fixed. As a result Scottish malt distilleries each have their own individual product flavour and the spirit is known by the name of the distillery. It also explains why great care is taken when replacing plant, particularly stills, to ensure that the new plant is identical in all respects to the original one.

There is a story about a distillery where a piece of equipment was accidently dropped on a still causing a large dent in the side of the still; when that still had to be replaced, a copper smith was instructed to build an identical still with an identical dent.

Reflux

When the liquid in a still comes to the boil, the body of the still is filled with vapour which has the composition of the equilibrium vapour which we can look up in tables. At this point there are two possibilities, all of the vapour can be removed and condensed, in which case the liquid distillate will have the composition of the equilibrium vapour; more commonly, a quantity of the vapour will condense and flow back into the still. This liquid will bear the same relationship to the vapour as the vapour does to the original liquid. For example, suppose 1000 kilos of vapour is formed, if the original alcoholic strength in the still was 8% by volume (6.34% mas), the equilibrium vapour composition is 42.09% mas; accordingly there are 420.9 kilos of alcohol and 579.1 of water. If we assume that 20% of the vapour condenses, this means that 200 kilos will be condensed and will have a composition of 6.34% mas i.e. it will contain 12.68 kilograms of alcohol and 187.32 of water.

	VAPOUR	STG	ALC	WATER
	KG	% MAS	KG	KG
VAPOUR REFLUX	1000	42.09	420.9	579.1
AT 20%	200	6.34	12.68	187.32
NET VAPOUR	800	51.03	408.22	391.78

We end up with 800 kilos of vapour containing 408.22 of alcohol, which is then condensed and collected in the receiver.

This results in the alcoholic content of the vapour increasing from 42.09% mas to 51.3% mas, and so it is clear that the degree of reflux has a significant impact on the distillate strength. Accordingly, if a still is filled with 8000 litres of wash at 8% alcohol by volume, the impact of reflux is given in the following table. Assuming that the distillation will be terminated at the distillate strength of 1% by volume, this value was used for the figures provided.

Reflux %	Low Wines Strength % by volume	Low Wines Litres
0	18.24	3455
5	19.08	3305
10	19.82	3184
15	20.66	3058
20	21.67	2905
25	22.78	2769
30	23.96	2628
35	25.56	2464
40	27.13	2324
45	29.23	2157
50	31.58	1996

In a Scottish type wash still, there is no control over the reflux rate which could therefore be described as natural reflux. The items which influence reflux are those which influence the cooling effect of the surface of all parts of the still from which condensate can flow back into the still. This would include the following:

- the available surface area
- the external temperature
- rate of distillation
- whether the lyne arm slopes upwards or downwards

These are influenced by the number of stills in the still house and the method of heating the stills. For example, if the stills are directly heated by a furnace, heat will travel through the copper; copper, being a very good conductor of heat, will tend to minimise the amount of reflux. Also, the temperature inside the still house where there is direct firing is liable to be much higher than in the case of indirect firing, and an enclosed still house where the condensers are inside with a large number of small direct fired stills will have a greatly reduced rate of reflux.

In addition to reflux, the alcoholic strength of the low wines is also influenced by the point at which distillation is ended. It is impossible to make a complete separation of water and alcohol by distillation only, and so a suitable cut off point in the distillation must be chosen. It is normal in the industry to terminate the distillation when the alcoholic strength of the distillate comes down to 1%. This being the equilibrium vapour composition of the liquid in the still, which is equivalent to the alcoholic strength in the still of approximately 0.1% (at this point in the equilibrium vapour curve, the vapour composition is approximately ten times that of the liquid). Where the still is fired by a furnace, it is impossible to stop heating at a given point in time, and whenever the fire is drawn out, there will be a residual degree of heat causing the distillation to continue for some time leading to more low strength spirit, both increasing the volume and decreasing the alcoholic strength of the low wines. It is clear that in the Scottish double distillation system, these differences play a significant role in determining the flavour characteristics of the final product.

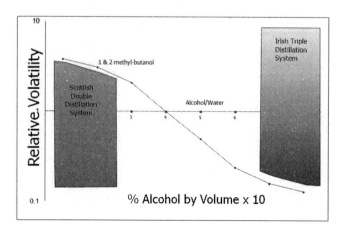

On this graph, the alcohol water composition from 1-90% is represented by a horizontal red line and shows the condition where the relative volatility in an alcohol/water mixture is 1. The blue curve represents the relative volatility of 1- and 2-methyl butanol; these are two of the main congeners in whiskey but laboratory experimentation has shown that they provide reliable markers for whatever additional substances are responsible for unpleasant taste. It should be noted that the vertical axis is logarithmic. From this it is obvious that if a pot still which contains liquid at 40% ABV, unpleasant flavours distil off and so this be avoided. For this reason, the Scottish malt whisky process normally begins with an alcoholic strength in the spirit still of 25% volume or less, this is the starting strength of the content of the spirit still but clearly it will diminish during the distillation process. It could be argued that the lower the value for this strength, the better the result in terms of final product quality.

Alternatively, in the Irish 3-stage process, the spirit still is charged with about 75% alcohol by volume. The strength will diminish during distillation, but in this process, only slightly. It can be seen that the Scotch and Irish processes are roughly equidistant from the danger point of 40%, but in opposite directions.

As already discussed, the Scotch system depends on collecting the low wines from a batch of wash and adding that to the recycled foreshots and feints from the previous distillation. This material is then charged into the spirit still, and given that the alcohol content of the final product must match the alcohol introduced to the system via the low wines less a very small percentage to allow for losses, the process is essentially inflexible and the charge in the spirit still must represent anything from 130% to 200% of the alcohol content of the low wines. Once again this is influenced by the reflux ratios. In many ways the inflexibility of the Scotch system is its strength, in that it results in each malt distillery producing a consistent product unique to that individual distillery and different from all others. The inflexibility, however, does not cater for either product improvement or process development. By contrast, the Irish system uses reflux to enable the necessary high strength of the final product to be obtained, and whilst in the traditional process the line arm was immersed in a tank of cold water and the reflux returned to the pot via the so-called foul pipe, this was done without any particular control. For this reason, in newer designs for the traditional Irish process, a line arm condenser normally of the multi-tubular variety has a system for adjusting the level of reflux so that required alcoholic strengths in the various distillates can be obtained.

The fermented wash contains water and alcohol and a number of congeners including organic acid, higher alcohols, esters etc. It might be believed that whiskey distillation simply amounts to obtaining virtually all of the alcohol as well as all of the other volatile materials; this is not the case. It was the original thought when Coffey designed his continuous still in 1830, but it was quickly shown that distillates of that type were vastly different from distillate made from pot stills. This is because pot stills involve boiling liquids for a number of hours and recycling selected fractions. This allows the minority constituents to react producing a whole range of additional flavoured products.

Some of these are flavour contributors or flavour enhancers which find their way into the final product. The main difference between distillation in a Coffey still and that in pot stills even allowing for the different final product strength (Coffey still 94.8%, Irish pot still 86%) is that wash is processed through a Coffey Still in approximately five minutes, whereas the wash distillation in an Irish whiskey pot still takes a number of hours. In the case of John Jameson, it was 13 hours 40 minutes. During this time, wash undergoes a cooking process as happens if a piece of ham and possibly some cabbage were boiled for an hour or so. The flavour change is well-recognised, and since fermented wash contains an equivalent number of organic materials, it is hardly surprising that during the boiling, changes take place and as in the case of bacon and cabbage these are mainly beneficial changes. In the Irish system, distillates are normally collected as strong and weak fractions and there is a considerable degree of recycling in which different fractions meet and are boiled together giving the opportunity for further flavour development. Whiskey distillation comprises a number of different processes with the following objectives:

- Wash distillation – in which alcohol and other volatile components are separated from water, the residues of yeast, other insoluble matter, non-fermentable materials etc.
- Distillation of low wines and subsequent recycled fractions to create a mixture of feints of alcoholic strength of about 75% by volume for further distillation.
- Recovery of alcohol from the remaining weak fractions.

Because the spirit still is charged with feints at a high alcoholic strength and because spirit stills were traditionally direct fired, the content of the still would reduce rapidly during distillations approaching a dangerous low-level situation. For this reason, it is practice to add further strong low wines to the spirit still. This causes a short interruption in distillation while the fraction is added and the still is brought back to the boil. Once again this allows fractions of different origins to be boiled together creating additional opportunities for flavour formation. Because of the large number of different recycled fractions in the Irish process, the number of ways in which this can be varied is quite large and this explains why whiskeys from the three remaining Republic of Ireland distilleries which were in production until the late 1960s each had their individual flavour and consequent strong brand loyalty at consumer level. This also explains why when Coffey developed his still around 1830, it was totally shunned by all the Irish distillers whose total sales in England and elsewhere then exceeded those of Scotch, and why the distillers recognised that their pot still process delivered a product of distinctive taste and one which was widely consumed.

The research department of Dutch Company, Naarden International, have compiled a list of substances found in whiskeys by a number of analysts throughout the world, and it found that most whiskeys contained almost 400 different substances; some or all of which contribute at some level to the final product flavour. Of these substances are 9 different higher alcohols, 5 different sugars, 125 different esters, 13 different sulphur compounds, 41 different compounds containing nitrogen, 23 ketones, 30 aldehydes, 4 lactones, and a number of organic acids. This accounts for about 300 of the 400 constituents.

It is noted that the analysis shows that whiskey contains a large amount of substances called esters. Esters are present in most fruits and play a major part in creating the flavour. An ester is formed when an organic acid combines with an alcohol. Two main acids, acetic and lactic, are formed during fermentation and ethanol, as well as small amounts of other higher alcohols of which there are reported to be nine, are also formed. The reaction in which an acid and alcohol are combined happens very easily in the presence of large amounts of water, but the process reverses very easily also. However, esters are very stable in stronger alcoholic mixtures and so, in a pot still, some of the ester formed in the liquid during boiling can be immediately distilled in to the much stronger distillate where it remains stable. This is but one example of how a pot still works in distilling whiskey.

All of the above refers to the Scotch Malt process which was also the way that Irish whiskey was distilled prior to the development of the mixed cereal system using unmalted barley. This general technique is still used to produce brandy and rum. As already stated, the adoption of the mixed cereal process in Ireland required an alternative pot still distillation method so as to provide satisfactory results. There were three distinct stages: wash was distilled into low wines, low wines into feints and feints into new whiskey. This was achieved by separating the distillate from the pot stills into strong and weak fractions and treating the two differently. It also included different patterns of recycling of the various fractions and given that there were more fractions to recycle, the taste options of the final product differed considerably. In the case of the wash stills, low wines were separated into strong and weak low wines. From there on the strong and weak fractions were treated differently. In particular, new whiskey was distilled from strong feints at 69% ABV with the addition of a small proportion of strong low wines. The first runnings from the spirit still were called first shot. They were brilliantly clear and the quantity was small. In fact, they probably consisted mainly of the rinsing of the residues from the previous distillation from the condenser. The stills were fitted with reflux condensers where a proportion of the vapour in the line arm was condensed and returned to the liquid in the still through a so-called foul pipe. This increased the alcoholic strength of the distillate and contributed towards the high alcoholic strength in the final product.

In the traditional system the rate of reflux was not controlled at any specific value, but it is obviously advantageous to be able to do this, and it was adopted later. The feints still was used mainly to recover alcohol from the weak fractions; it was very energy intensive and it was believed that the relatively small quantity of strong feints produced from this still had an unpleasant taste, and was thought to contribute to some of the negative factors identified in the final product; in particular it was a bitter element in the taste and had an incompatibility with ice.

In a research programme in the late 1960s working towards the building of the new Midleton distillery, it was decided to replace the function of the feints still with a column which could recover the alcohol from the weak fractions without the development of the already discussed unpleasant taste elements, and would do so in a much more energy efficient manner. This type of still where a column is introduced to a group of pot stills is called a 'Hybrid Still'. Provided the final distillation is by pot still, the distillate can be defined as 'New Make Pot Still Whiskey', and if there are three stages in the distillation process the product can be described as 'Triple Distilled'.

In the two-stage process, the wash still is charged with a mixture of low wines, foreshots and feints, the foreshots and feints being recycled fractions from the previous distillation. The alcoholic strength in the spirit still may vary from just over 25% ABV down to the upper teens. Precisely what the strength is, plays a major role in defining the taste characteristics of the final product. When distillation commences, foreshots distil over first and can be identified by the formation of a blue opalescence on the addition of water. Once the foreshots have distilled off, and they would normally represent about 4% of the total throughput, new whiskey or, as they call it in Scotland, spirit is distilled over; this is what was described as the heart of the distillation. As distillation continues the alcoholic strength of the distillate gradually diminishes. When the distillate strength reaches a pre-determined level, the remainder of the distillate, called feints is directed to the foreshots, low wines and feints tank for recycling.

It is clear that the amount of alcohol in the distillation of new whiskey is equal to the alcohol present in the initial charge of low wines, less a very small amount accounted for by the small residue of alcohol in the spent wash and spent lees. Current regulations for whiskey state that: a spirit may not be referred to as whiskey until it has been matured in wood for at least three years (meaning 36 months). For this reason, the Scots call it spirit and the Irish call it new whiskey.

	Irish Pot Still Whiskey	Scottish Malt Whisky
Raw Material	Mixture of malt and unmalted barley	100% Malt
Distillation Stages	3	2
Recycling	Strong and weak fractions	Foreshots and feints only
Spirit Still Charge strength	69% ABV	20-25% ABV
Control reflux	Yes	No
Final Distillate	86%ABV	69% ABV

Chapter 9
The Skill of Distilling Crosses the Atlantic

Atlant Whiskey is produced by brewing a mixture of cereals all, or part, of which is malt to form Wort which is then fermented by yeast. The fermented wort is distilled and the final distillate matured in a wooden cask. The aspects which impact on the flavour of the whiskey are as follows –

- Choice of cereals
- Fermentation
- Distillation
- Maturation
- Local conditions

Local conditions include water quality, ambient temperature and humidity, air-borne bacteria, pollens etc. Whiskeys, traditionally made in Ireland and Scotland, were carried to the new world by immigrants. Elsewhere, many countries, notably Japan, produced whiskeys of a scotch-type mainly for consumption by their indigenous populations. Not all of these whiskeys are produced according to the regulations of either the European Union or the United States. Also, some contain bulk product imported from Scotland, Ireland or elsewhere which plays some part in bringing their indigenous product closer in taste qualities to what is internationally understood as whiskey.

New world whiskeys differ in taste qualities from those of Scotland and Ireland mainly because they have had to adapt to new raw materials and different ambient conditions. For example, when the Irish arrived initially in the eastern seaboard of the United States, they found rye to be closest to the barley that they were used to, particularly since it could be malted. So, in states like Maryland and Pennsylvania, rye whiskey was distilled. Eventually a dispute arose about taxation which the distillers regarded as unfair, and like all good Americans when they had a problem, they moved westwards and finally settled in Kentucky. Here, there were two problems; the widely available cereal was maize (which the Americans call corn) and so they had to learn to use that as a main starting material with small amounts of malt either from barley or rye. Another problem was that the water in Kentucky is exceptionally hard. They learned how to deal with the first by making what was called Bourbon whiskey, originally produced in Bourbon County in Kentucky, in which the mash bill contained at least 51% maize. The remaining balance was made up of malted and unmalted barley and/or rye. The second problem was that of the hard water for which they devised a process described as back slopping in which the clarified spent wash which the Americans called thin stillage is added to the brew water to adjust the pH to about 5.6, ideal for distilling.

Both of these changes impacted the product flavour. Not all American whiskeys are produced in Bourbon County of Kentucky but Bourbon has now become a name for a type of whiskey made in other parts of Kentucky and elsewhere. A different type of whiskey is made in Tennessee and there is also Rye Whiskey.

Whiskey became so popular in the United States that in the 1920s they decided to ban it altogether except for medical reasons.

The so called 'prohibition' was a huge mistake and even today some criminal activity still has its origins in prohibition.

It is the responsibility of those who govern a country to enact laws to protect the people whom they have been elected to represent, but there are also those who wish to change society into some sort of ideal. Unless this ideal is shared by the vast majority of the population, any laws designed to create it are doomed to failure. Prohibition was an excellent example of this.

The 18th Amendment to the U.S. Constitution proposed a total ban on the manufacture, sales and transportation of alcoholic liquor. Alcoholic liquor was defined as that containing more than 0.5% alcohol. Under this amendment, owning any equipment designed for the production of liquor was also an offence punishable by a jail term. The Volstead Act was proposed in 1919, and one year's notice was given such that it came into effect on January 16th 1920 as the 18th Amendment.

It is easily understood how this could have come about because we have all heard stories of parents, usually male, who drink excessively. Usually, they return home in a drunken state, having spent a disproportionate amount of the family's modest budget. Such individuals often attack and beat up their wives or partners and scare their children or, even worse, abuse them.

Let us get one thing straight from the start. People abuse alcohol; alcohol does not abuse people. The alcohol referred to is ethyl alcohol (otherwise known as ethanol, or 1-methylcarbinol). It is the effective ingredient in all beers, wines and spirits and has well-known physiological effects. A minority of people (estimated to be in the region of 5%) have an addictive reaction to alcohol and such people should not consume it at any time. Some people abuse alcohol by over-indulgence or by using it irresponsibly, sometimes this abuse is a symptom of other problems. For the vast majority, taking alcohol in the form of whiskey or any other alcoholic drink is an enjoyable, social and life enhancing experience, and there is well substantiated evidence that it can be beneficial to health.

As such, prohibition sought to deprive the vast majority of the population of what was for them, a life enhancing experience. It also deprived those who had been involved in production, distribution, marketing and selling alcoholic products, of their livelihood. There were, however, some exclusions. The production of alcohol was permitted under strict control exclusively for medical purposes, and people could obtain liquor if prescribed by a medical practitioner. The actual drinking of alcoholic liquor was not in fact an offence and so people who stored up liquor in advance of prohibition coming into effect were free to enjoy it personally but not to sell it.

The absence of any legal ways of obtaining liquor, coupled with the obvious demand, was an opportunity for gangsters. It is said that some organised crime in America, even today, has its roots in prohibition. Liquor was obtained from the Caribbean by so called 'rum runners' and a row of old ships, called the 'Rum Row' was kept at anchor just outside American territorial waters to act as floating liquor stores. The liquor was obtained by people in small fishing boats and in some instances floated ashore in the wooden crates which were used before the development of corrugated cartons. The rum runners did not only carry rum. There are reports of at least one Caribbean island importing much more Scotch whisky than could possibly be consumed by its population. Whiskey was also smuggled in from Canada, although, wishing to behave like a good neighbour, the Canadian Government imposed restrictions on the purchase of liquor, which made it difficult for any individual to buy liquor other than for his or her own use.

Illegal drinking was not limited to speakeasies and much of it happened at home. There are reports that the importation of cocktail shakers reached an all-time high during the prohibition years. Some people produced their own liquor or bought from illegal and, therefore, doubtful sources. In addition to smuggling, there were small illegal distilleries producing moonshine or bath tub gin. Such liquor was often very crude and had to be mixed with other things to make it palatable. This began the practice of taking drinks as cocktails as evidenced by the importation of cocktail shakers. Obtaining liquor from doubtful sources had its downside because ethyl alcohol in drinks is part of a family of alcohols and its nearest neighbour is methanol or methyl alcohol. Some people, who probably knew no better, assumed it to be the same as alcohol, but methanol causes blindness and in larger quantities, death. I wonder if the years in question were associated with an increase in cases of blindness?

Californian wine producers, having their livelihood removed by prohibition, resorted to producing a grape juice extract called Vine-Glo. This was, of course, non-alcoholic but it was soon found that by adding some sugar and a little water, alcohol would be produced converting the legal Vine-Glo into something approaching wine, which was illegal. Near beer was a non-alcoholic beer which was promoted to replace normal beer, and there is a story that New York Mayor, Fiorello La Guardia, purchased some near beer and also some malt extract, both of which were widely and legally on sale. After mixing them and allowing the mixture to stand for some time, it acquired an illegal content of greater than 2% alcohol.

There was a gradual realisation that prohibition was not delivering the honest upright sober society to which its supporters aspired, and whilst some believed that stronger and more comprehensive enforcement was necessary, a movement was led by Pauline Sabin to campaign for the repeal of the Volstead Act. Pauline was particularly concerned by the negative attitudes abroad to America under prohibition, but the main thrust of public opinion came from taxation. The ending of the Government revenue stream from the production, distribution and legal sales of alcoholic beverages left a significant hole in tax take, which had to be made up by increasing taxation on the population at large and nobody likes having to pay extra tax. On the other hand, the supporters of prohibition had one trump card – at that time no constitutional amendment had ever been repealed, and so there was no precedent. We all know how politicians like precedents.

Prohibition was ended by the passing of the 21st amendment on the 7th of April 1933. Two points arise – a law which inhibits or denies the normal rights of the vast majority in an effort to modify the behaviour of a minority is bad law, and a law which criminalises otherwise honest upright citizens is a bad law. I hope future legislators will keep these points in mind.

Canada benefitted from prohibition in the U.S. as many of the distillers moved over the border and set up there. This way the skills were preserved so that when prohibition was ultimately repealed in 1933. Qualified distillers were able to move south to the U.S. to re-start the industry. During prohibition, the Canadian government set up controls to help avoid Canadian-produced whiskies being smuggled over the border to the U.S.

Whisky production in Canada is very different from that of Ireland or Scotland. Barley grows there as well as maize and rye. They use a process which they call pre-blending, in which the product is built up starting with neutral alcohol produced from maize, with the addition of pot still distillates derived mainly from rye. The final product is blended prior to being filled into casks for what is normally a four-year maturation period.

Chapter 10
The Development of
Irish Whiskey

Over the years Irish whiskey developed from small personal stills in the kitchen of a big house, a back yard or attached to an inn or hostelry to the massive exporting industry it is today. Many of the changes which brought this about were as a consequence of regulation beginning in 1661 when King James introduced the first ever excise duty on spirits with the twin but conflicting objectives of diminishing drunkenness and raising funds to finance his many wars.

The rate was of four old pence per gallon of whiskey, and this started a worldwide trend of raising excise duty on distilled spirits. The whole thing was a bit foolhardy then because there was no way of measuring the alcoholic strength of the whisky, and to raise tax on the volume of whiskey without reference to the alcoholic strength is nonsense. There was only one way of checking the strength of whiskey then. It was mixed with gunpowder and if the mixture burned with a blue flame, the whiskey was deemed to be '100% proof perfect', thus indicating that no excess water had been added. This procedure may have been adequate for commercial transactions but it was totally inadequate for excise purposes where transparency was and still is the order of the day.

The imposition of excise duty put a big responsibility on the revenue authorities whose job was to measure the actual amounts of whiskey produced and to impose and collect the necessary taxes; for this reason they were referred to as 'Gaugers'. The first objective was to increase the size of each operation and, as a result, bring about a reduction in the number of plants that had to be visited and controlled. Distilleries had to be licensed and stills containing 400 gallons or more had to be registered. In the mid-18th century, there were about 1000 distilleries, a very large number of which had stills smaller than the specified 400 gallons and which were unable to become registered. This left them few options; they could invest in larger equipment or give up altogether. Many of those did neither, but continued to distil illegally, and their product coming from a small still was called poitín, the Irish word for such a still. Until today, illegal poitín is distilled and occasionally an operation is discovered by the authorities, who impound materials and equipment. If they can be found, these illegal distillers are prosecuted. These activities usually take place in remote areas. Uninhabited islands in places like Lough Corrib or Clew Bay are often chosen. One recent development which greatly assisted the poitín distillers was bottled gas because hitherto smoke from the fire under the still was a giveaway. I have also heard stories of fishermen who kept the equipment when not in use in the sea like a lobster pot which could be retrieved at short notice for a batch of distillation and then returned to the seabed. There is such romance and folklore about distilling poitín that in recent times there has been a development where legally produced poitín products are marketed as such.

Returning to the licensed distillers, there being no satisfactory way of measuring the amount of whiskey produced since the strength could not be determined; a method was devised to relate the whiskey obtained from the amount of malt used in its production, it being comparatively easier to measure malt usage. At that stage Irish whiskey was distilled from 100% malt and as such a complicated calculation was devised which related the malt used to the whiskey production and thence to the duty payable. This was called the malt tax.

Of all the impositions from the authorities to find ways of securing the revenue, the one which had most impact in Ireland was the malt tax. No one likes to pay tax and so to minimise the effect of the malt tax, the distillers found a way to obtain a satisfactory fermentation using a mixture of malted and unmalted barley. However, when they tried to distil it using the traditional two-stage process, they did not obtain satisfactory results. What followed must have involved a good deal of trial and error, but they finally developed a process in which distillation took place in three stages and where the final distillate strength was approximately 86% by volume. This is how traditional Irish whiskey is produced today and is yet another unique element in the production of Irish whiskey.

None of these things happened in Scotland because although the union of the crowns took place in 1603, the union of parliament did not occur until 1707. The Scottish distilleries were mainly located in remote areas of the

Highlands and islands. Consequently the Scottish Parliament was slow or even reluctant to propose new regulations coming from England.

The difficulties related to the collection of excise duty continued until 1816 when the Hydrometer, invented by Bartholomew Sikes in 1802, an instrument for the accurate measurement of alcohol was enshrined into law. For the first time Sikes defined 'Proof Spirit' as:

"That mixture of alcohol and water which weighs 12/13ths of the same volume of water when these are measured at 51^0F (equivalent to 56.97 % VOL at 20^0C)."

The instrument comes with a set of weights, one of which can be hung on the lower part of the stem of the hydrometer. The temperature of the liquid to be tested is recorded. The hydrometer is then fitted with the appropriate weight so that the hydrometer will float. The strength is determined by a combination of reading the scale on the hydrometer stem and the value of the weight which had been attached.

The Sikes Hydrometer was based on the principle that alcohol weighs only about 80% of the same volume of water and that the weight a fixed volume of an alcohol-water mixture, called the specific gravity, can be used to determine the alcoholic content. The instrument depends upon the law of floatation which can be illustrated as follows: when a ship afloat on the sea water is pushed aside to accommodate the shape of its hull, this is called displacement and it so happens that the weight of the water displaced is exactly equal to the weight of the ship.

The Jonathan Swift, named after the famous Irish author, is the most modern high-speed car ferry servicing the route between Ireland and Great Britain, a journey which takes only 1 hour and 49 minutes. This vessel has a capacity for 189 cars as well as trucks and other commercial vehicles. The average family car weighs about two tonnes and as each car drives on to one of the car decks, an additional two tonnes of water is displaced until the maximum permitted amount is reached. It is obvious that as the ship is loaded it goes deeper into the water, and there are lines painted on the side of the hull indicating the maximum safe depth.

When the Sikes Hydrometer is in use, the volume of liquid displaced can be read from the stem of the instrument and the weight is equal to the weight of the instrument itself and whatever weight has been added to it. The temperature is read using the Fahrenheit scale. The page on the Sikes tables' equivalent to the temperature of the sample is referred to and the alcoholic strength in degrees under or over proof are read off opposite the indication. This process was accurate and equally accessible to the excise officer and to the trader, so that the strength of any sample of spirit could be tested by both and agreed upon. The quantity of spirit then could be calculated in proof gallons. That was the theoretical volume the spirit would occupy if its alcoholic strength was precisely 100^0 proof. This way alcohol duty was raised on the basis of the proof gallon.

The industrialisation of whiskey production brought a number of developments. With much larger distilleries, whiskey had to be stored, transported, and even exported. At that time, wooden casks were about the only containers available. They came mainly from Spain, containing sherry and other wines. It was discovered that whiskey, which had been in a cask for some time, acquired a beautiful amber colour from the wood (and to some extent from the sherry or whatever had previously been contained in the cask). The whiskey became smoother and more pleasing to the palate. Maturation in oak soon became an essential part of whiskey production and is now enshrined in law.

The involvement of excise officers in the production of whiskey brought about a whole range of regulations, much of which happened during the 18th Century. Initially, whiskey distillation was a local or even domestic pastime, and as production units got larger, transportation difficulties meant that the products of each distillery were consumed within a relatively small radius. As units got larger, rivers were used for motive power but still there were limits as to where the products could be transported.

From then on, Irish whiskey underwent a number of changes. The malt tax in 1785 heralded the introduction of mixed cereal and a consequent development of triple distillation. Simultaneously, steam engines became available and distilleries were no longer required to be located next to rivers with a sufficiently large flow of water to drive a water wheel which would provide motive power for the entire distillery. These two developments made it possible for distilleries to become larger and to move as close as possible to the main export market, England. As a result, nearly 20 distilleries appeared in Dublin, near to the port, and a potential workforce. Similarly, in Cork, a group of distilleries appeared which eventually merged to form Cork Distilleries Ltd.

Sales of Jameson whiskey began to grow, mainly due to the large English market nearby where brandy, which had been the main spirit drink in England, was gradually being replaced by Irish whiskey. Sales of Irish whiskey in England got a boost during the 1800s when around 1850 the parasitic disease *Phylloxera* attacked the French vines bringing about a shortage of wine and consequently a shortage of Brandy.

Throughout the 1800s, Irish whiskey was the world number one in which the main markets were England and the United States.

Aenaes Coffey, former Irish excise officer, working in Dublin, invented a continuous still which did three things that appeared to be beneficial. First of all, it was operated by steam which was more economical to produce and minimised the labour requirements. Next, having observed that distilling at higher strength from about 69%-86% by volume greatly improved the whiskey taste quality; it seemed a logical step that by distilling at an even higher strength of just over 94% by volume, further improvements would be achieved. Sadly, this transpired not to be the case and the so-produced whiskey was considerably milder in taste leading to the idea that it did not require maturation. That too was not to be the case. The Irish whiskey distillers who were then on the crest of a wave did not want to take any risks by the introduction of alternative production methods, and Coffey went to England and began manufacturing his patent still in 1830, selling to gin distillers and later to Scotch whisky distillers where they made a totally different product called grain whiskey which was used almost exclusively for blending purposes.

By the early 20th century, Blended Scotch Whisky took off and exceeded sales of Irish whiskey by 1914. Scotch whisky also spread into export markets on a worldwide basis.

From the early 1900s onwards, Irish whiskey went through bad times. First there were 'The Troubles', and then the two World Wars as well as Irish independence and prohibition in the United States. All of these combined to create a very difficult time for Irish whiskey.

By the 1950s, there were only five companies producing Irish whiskey and during this time Tullamore and Kilbeggan went to the wall leaving Jameson and Powers in Dublin and Cork Distilleries Co. in Cork. The two Dublin distilleries were producing mainly for the domestic market, but Jameson had managed to retain a small share of export markets. In Cork Distilleries they developed Cork Dry Gin which was a most successful product commanding over 80% of the gin market, which at that time was considerable. Unlike whiskey, gin does not require maturation and Cork Dry Gin became a very profitable enterprise.

Bushmills Distillery had been operating in Northern Ireland for many years. They produced a malt whiskey which was made from 100% malt and distilled in three stages. They also produced Scotch-type grain whiskey and the blended product was very successful in Ireland and they also had a healthy export business.

At this time, English breweries were merging to form large groups, and one such group, Bass Charrington, bought Bushmills Distillery. There was a fear that the next target would be Cork Distilleries mainly because of their very successful gin. This motivated the other Irish distilleries to join with Cork Distilleries to form a group which would be sufficiently strong to resist any takeover from English breweries. It was also judged that working together as a group, they would have an opportunity to make inroads into export markets which were recognised to be the way forward. This came about in 1966 when The United Distillers of Ireland was formed, having the initials UDI. However, about the same time, Ian Smith in Rhodesia was proposing a unilateral declaration of independence and the initials UDI were adopted by the media. As a result, the name of the new Irish company was quickly changed to Irish Distillers Ltd.

The larger recourses of the group members enabled a combined marketing and exporting department to be set up under modern lines, as well as combined production activities such as bottling and warehousing. Of prime importance was to research the whiskey production process with a view to improving the product taste and streamlining the production methods to give enhanced operational efficiency.

Working as a group, research was undertaken into production methods and eventually one single new distillery was planned at Midleton, Co Cork. This was described as a distillery complex because it had been designed to replicate all the products of the group. The fact that these products remain on the market today is evidence that this approach was successful. Research work was undertaken on all the processes involved including brewing, distilling and maturation, and substantial improvements in the techniques used for these processes were achieved and built into the design of the new Midleton Distillery. Of particular note was distillation because it was shown in the research that the very distinct taste characteristics of each product were produced by details as to how the distillation process was operated. In the distillation process the hybrid still was developed. This introduced a column still together with the pot stills, using the column still to recover alcohol from the weak fractions which is both time consuming and expensive to do in pot stills. It was also found that distilling weak fractions in pot stills generated unpleasant flavours, particularly a certain bitterness which was universally disliked and which was accentuated in the presence of ice.

In a pot still distillation, the alcoholic fractions are boiled and the resultant vapour passes up the neck and into the condenser where the vapour becomes liquid and as we know the alcoholic strength of the distillate diminishes during the operation. Normally we want to remove substantially all of the alcohol from the content of the pot, and to do so, distillation is stopped when the distillate strength is 1%. At this level the relative volatility of alcohol in an alcohol/water mixture is about x10, leaving the content of the pot with 0.1% alcohol by volume.

The traditional Irish three-stage process requires the still for the final distillation to be charged at about 79% alcohol by volume to give a distillate strength of about 86% A.B.V., and this is quite a challenge using only pot stills. As a result, a number of steps are taken to make this possible.

1. The lyne arms are cooled and an amount of condensate returned to the still via a so-called 'foul pipe'. This has the effect of increasing the strength of the distillate (Today this can be a multi-tubular condenser and the flow through the foul pipe is controlled so as to give the required distillate strength).

2. The early part of each distillation when the spirit is at its strongest goes towards the final product, and the weak fractions are re-distilled in the feints still to produce a small amount of strong spirit which is added into final product stream and the balance is returned to the feints still for further distillation.

The boiling of the liquids in the pot stills is beneficial to the final product flavour and complexity, just like in cooking when bacon and cabbage. When these are boiled in a pot there are beneficial changes in taste, but we all know that, particularly cabbage which is boiled for too long develops bitter unpleasant flavours. Likewise, when weak alcoholic fractions, which contain a complex mixture of natural organic substances, and which like cabbage, contain traces of sulphur, are boiled for a prolonged period as happens in the feints still, bitter unpleasant flavours also result.

The solution lies with developments following the column still patented by the Irishman, Aeneas Coffey. In the column still the alcoholic liquid is processed within about five minutes giving virtually no cooking effect. Furthermore, a column still has the capability of distilling liquid containing only two or three percent alcohol into high strength spirit of 80% A.B.V. or more in one single pass. To sum up, a column has the capacity to recover alcohol from weak fractions without the development of flavours of any kind. Furthermore, the column still is highly energy efficient and takes over at a point when the pot stills become progressively more energy inefficient.

In the hybrid still, the column is positioned to replace the feints still and as such the final distillation is by pot still. In this case the regulations allow the final product to be described 'pot still', and after at least three years maturation in wood, 'Pot still Whiskey'.

We know that whiskey must be matured for at least three years, but pot still whiskey takes much longer to acquire true drinking quality. We all remember the old Jameson slogan: 'Not a drop is sold till it is seven years old', and in more recent times the preferred age has been increased to ten or more years. It is very difficult to run a business if you have to plan production for sales ten years away and the answer is blending.

When Coffey invented his two-column still, the Scotch whisky industry quickly adopted it and produced what they called 'grain whisky'. This kind of whisky matures within three years and when it is blended with older malt whisky, it produces what they call 'blended whisky'. This type of whisky represents the vast majority of Scotch whiskies and enabled the rapid growth of Scotch whisky worldwide starting at the beginning of the twentieth century. The research team in Irish distillers recognised the need for a similar approach, but they quickly found that Scotch type grain whisky is not compatible with Irish pot still whiskey and set about developing a more suitable grain whiskey. The result was Irish light grain. This was produced from a mash of barley saccharified with about 20% malt, which after fermentation was distilled in a three-column still. This produced a suitable grain whiskey which matured in three years and since it was distilled in three columns, it could be described as 'triple distilled'.

Irish regulations do not require the fact that a whiskey is a blend (of pot still and light grain) to be declared as such, and it can merely be described as triple distilled Irish whiskey. This is the road ahead and the vast majority of Irish whiskey exports are produced this way.

Chapter 11
Early Distillation, Gin and Fortified Wines

When whiskey was first distilled, due to the simple nature of the distillation process at that time, the early product had a fairly rough taste. For this reason, things were added to it to make it more palatable. In Ireland, early recipes for *Uisce Beatha* show that the fresh distillate was modified by the addition of saffron which gave it a beautiful orange/amber colour, not unlike the colour of whiskey today and also nutmeg, clove, cinnamon, aniseed, caraway and coriander. At that time, Irish *Uisce Beatha* was rated to be one of the best in flavour and general taste characteristics.

In the meantime, the art of distillation spread to southern England and Northern Europe where to soften the taste of the spirit, they added juniper, sugar and spices such as angelica cassia and coriander and this became the basis of gin. Today, gin has benefitted from large improvements into distillation methods including the use of multi-column stills which are a development from the original Coffey design, and as such sugar was eliminated from the formulation, enabling gin to be called dry gin. Unlike whiskey, gin does not require maturation and is ready to drink almost immediately after production. For this reason it is a very popular craft spirit, and craft gins are emerging in Europe and elsewhere.

Due to Spain's warm and sunny climate, grapes grow in prodigious numbers, producing large volumes of wine. To the North and East are Ireland, the United Kingdom and Scandinavia, all of which are too cold and too wet to grow grapes successfully in quantities suitable for wine making. Accordingly, we have one country with vast quantities of wine and several other countries relatively nearby where no wine is produced, but there is an obvious demand. The solution to this problem would be simply to export the wine to where there is a demand, but unfortunately, Spanish wines, especially the white ones, do not travel well and undergo oxidation during transit with extremely adverse consequences as far as flavour and aroma are concerned (Today this problem has been overcome by the addition of permitted amounts of sulphites).

The art of distillation developed particularly in Holland and spread throughout Europe. Dutch engineers travelled to France and helped to begin the Cognac industry there and then on to Spain where, near the town of Jerez de la Frontera, they taught Spaniards how to distil a portion of their wine and add back the distillate to more wine, bringing the alcoholic content from about 12% to 18%, invoking the anti-oxidant and preservative qualities of alcohol. The wine, called *Jerez* (pronounced 'Hereth') was anglicised to Sherry. Depending on precisely how the maturation process was operated, sherry could be dark-coloured and sweet, and this was called Olorosso. Conversely, dry sherry called 'fino' is pale in colour and there are some intermediates, particularly amontillado which is amber-coloured medium sweet.

The newly fortified wine required some time to marry, and this was carried out in oak casks grouped together in a system called a *solera*. Here the wine was transferred from one cask to another and eventually there was a full cask of mature sherry. At that time the manufacturers chose not to get involved in bottling and simply exported the sherry in cask to the export markets, mainly Ireland, Britain and Scandinavia. Wine merchants locally bottled the sherry leaving the empty cask, which was then put up for sale. Whiskey distillers bought the empty casks which they then used to mature the whiskey.

Meanwhile, elsewhere in Europe, the practice of fortifying wine spread, first of all in Portugal, where in the Douro valley, distilled wine was added to fermenting grapes to produce a deep red-coloured wine and since this was near the town of Oporto, the wine was called Port. It is interesting to note that by adding the fortifying alcohol to the fermenting grapes at different times in the fermentation process, the final product could be either sweet or dry or somewhere in between. Some port is matured in bottle but the balance is matured in tall narrow oak casks which are referred to as port pipes and they too are sometimes used for maturing whiskey.

The fortification process was adopted on the island of Madeira to produce a fortified, sherry-like wine called Madeira and a similar wine in Italy is called Marsala. A large number of fortified wines, such as vermouth, Commandaria etc. are flavoured by the addition of wormwood and other substances. The name vermouth is actually derived from wormwood.

The Scotch and Irish whiskey producers worked with oak casks, mainly those which had previously produced sherry, until sometime in the 1950s when the Spanish government decided that there was considerable value to be added in Spain, if the sherry was bottled there also, and passed a regulation permitting sherry to be exported only in bottle. This would have created a serious problem for the distillers but they were saved by the fact that prohibition in the US had been repealed in 1933. The regulations for American Bourbon required it to be matured in new American Oak casks which had been internally charred and which could be used only once. This resulted in the availability of large numbers of American barrels which had previously contained Bourbon and which were quickly adopted by the whiskey industries of both Ireland and Scotland. This did not mean that the distillers had totally given up on sherry casks because whilst sherry was no longer exported in cask, new Iberian oak casks were used to contain sherry for approximately six months and then after emptying in Spain were available to be exported to the whiskey industries.

Chapter 12
Maturation

A whiskey maturation

Saffron is produced from the dried stigmas of the flower of *Crocus sativus* which grows in Spain, as well as in southern France and Italy. It is used as flavouring in some exotic dishes and has a bright orange colour. Saffron rice is one example, in which both flavour and colour play a part in the final product. It was also formerly used as a dye in the traditional orange-coloured Irish saffron kilt. Saffron has to be picked by hand, and as a result, in more recent times it has become very expensive, and has generally been replaced by less expensive products.

When Irish whiskey was first filled into wooden barrels, originally as a means of storage, the mellowing of the flavour and the extraction of colour from the wood was observed. This made it unnecessary to add botanicals to mellow the flavour or saffron to produce the orange/amber colour. From then onwards freshly distilled spirit, to which only water had been added, was filled into wooden casks and allowed to stand for a number of years to mature and develop colour. Today, spirit cannot be called whiskey until it has spent a specified number of years, usually three or four, in wooden barrels.

By far the most popular timber for whiskey barrels is oak, particularly American White Oak: *Quercus alba*. This comes from huge natural forests. It is a feature of natural afforestation that the trees grow close together, because after the mature timber has been cut down, thousands of acorns start to grow. These compete with one another to get access to light. This causes the trees to grow long and straight and not have many side branches. Oak is a slow growing tree, so when it is ready to be felled after what might be one hundred or more years, the trees have long straight trunks and virtually no side branches. At one cooperage I visited in Kentucky I saw a load of oak being delivered. The trunks were wide in diameter, straight and long – 40 feet or more.

The first stage in making barrels is to cut the trunks into sections using a large double circular saw. These sections – longer ones the length of staves and shorter ones for the heads – are then quartered vertically and then cut into lengths of equal thickness but varying widths. The lengths of oak are loosely stacked on pallets and placed out of doors to season, for at least one summer.

The seasoned staves are then shaped, by holding them against huge revolving abrasive disks. The inner surface is made concave and the outer, convex. Both sides are then tapered, top and bottom, and then the barrel can be built. The shaped staves are fitted into a former fixed to the floor, and held together by a few temporary trussing hoops, then the barrel is steamed. This makes the timber pliable and allows the tops of the staves to be brought together and held by a trussing hoop. The final hoops are then fitted and driven until the barrel is tight at which point the trussing hoops are removed. The barrel is then internally charred using a powerful gas flame. There are different levels of charring. Casks intended for wine are very lightly charred – a process called toasting. On the other hand, whiskey barrels are heavily charred producing a thick internal caramelised layer, which contributes both to the flavour and colour of the matured whiskey.

At the same time the heads are made. The short lengths of oak are fixed side by side using dowels to form a large enough piece, which is then shaped into a perfect circle of the right size. The hoops at each end of the barrel are loosened and the heads fitted into a specially cut groove in the cask called the croze. The hoops are then driven back into place to form a strong, leak proof container, which can be moved by rolling it on its bilge and stacked on its head. All internal surfaces are of oak, and the only other material is steel used for the external hoops. There is absolutely no glue, adhesive or alternative fixing material.

Spain is a country where grapes grow in abundance, and where vast quantities of wine are produced. Nearby, in Ireland and England as well as Scandinavia, vines do not grow successfully, therefore, there is no indigenous wine and consequently there is an obvious demand. We have Spain with an excess of wine and nearby countries wishing to obtain it, however there is one problem – the white wines produced predominantly in southern Spain do not appear to travel well because during the length of time it takes to ship the wine from Spain to the intended export market. Oxidation tends to occur rendering the wine from bitter, to entirely undrinkable.

When the art of distilling wine was known the Spanish wine producers found that by distilling some of the wine and adding the high strength distillate to more wine, a process called fortification. The final product was then matured in oak casks, in this case mainly Iberian Oak. This was found to make a pleasant wine-like drink which was sufficiently stable to be shipped to Ireland, Great Britain and Scandinavia. The process involved a 'Solera system' in which the wine was matured in a stack of oak casks and transferred according to the skill of the blender from one to another, until a final standard product was reached. Much of this happened around the ancient town of Jerez de la Frontera ('Jerez' in Spanish is pronounced 'Hereth' and this was anglicised to 'sherry'.) This development created a need for large quantities of oak casks and the Spaniards, who were already skilled at making casks, discovered that American oak imported as ballast in their ships returning from the new world was most suitable for casks. The producers of sherry did not include bottling as one of their skills, and so sherry was exported in cask, usually the final cask in each Solera system. The actual bottling was carried out by the importer in Ireland, Great Britain or elsewhere. As soon as the cask was emptied, it was put up for sale. Wooden casks were used for multiple purposes during these times, and many were sold on to Scottish and Irish distillers which was their main source of casks.

Following prohibition in the United States in 1933, the production of American whiskeys was regulated and for the main one, bourbon, the regulations stated that bourbon must be matured for a specified number of years in a new oak cask which has been internally charred. Typical bourbons are matured for four years after which the cask is for sale. This was fortuitous because in the mid-60s, the Spanish government enacted a regulation which required all sherry to be exported in bottle, severely restricting the availability of sherry casks to the distillers. It is still possible to obtain some sherry casks, but these are expensive. In general, in the whiskey industry bourbon casks are largely used for maturation, because they are of uniform size and suitable for stacking on their heads on palates and each cask can be used a number of times.

Maturation is one of these processes which is not totally understood. The basic facts are that changes in both the colour and the flavour of the product are observed; these are influenced by the type of cask, the size of cask, whatever it contained prior to being filled, and a number of other features such as the temperature, humidity and conditions in the warehouse. Choice of casks is as follows –

- American Barrels – nominal capacity of 180 litres, external height 813 mm, external bilge diameter 610 mm
- Butts – capacity approx. 550 Litres
- Hogsheads – capacity 255 Litres
- Dump Hogsheads – capacity 250 Litres, external height 813 mm, external bilge diameter 711 mm

American barrels, hogsheads and dumps, and today, even butts may be matured on their heads on pallets or on their bilges. Casks which are matured on their heads must have the bilge bung made of poplar, because unlike oak, poplar expands in both directions, so when it gets wet it makes a satisfactory seal. Butts are usually matured on their bilges, in which case a dunnage system is commonly used where a row of butts on the ground are covered with a pair of wooden batons, on top of which, there can be one or two tiers of hogsheads. It is common in the whiskey industry to use casks a number of times – up to four or five. In this case the original 'content' of the cask becomes progressively less important and the cask can be described as plain. Conversely first refills of casks which previously contained sherry or bourbon, or Port or Madeira, also impacts on the maturation. The original filling strength for Scottish malt whiskies was 11 over proof (63.5% volume), and grain whiskies 20 over proof (69% volume) respectively, and for Irish whiskey 25 over proof (71% by volume). It is now generally agreed that 71% is far too high and that no real maturation happens until the strength gradually works its way down into the 60s. Approval to do this coincided approximately with the reduction of the minimum maturation age for Irish whiskey from 5 years to 3 years. Most whiskeys are now placed in casks at 63.5% volume. In warehouses with a high natural humidity there is a reduction during maturation of the alcoholic strength whilst the volume remains relatively constant. Conversely, in low humidity warehouses the alcohol strength remains more or less constant but there is a loss of volume. In both these situations, in terms of alcohol, there is an annual loss of 2%, the so-called 'Angel's share'. Everyone is concerned about the alcohol loss, but what they don't consider is that new whiskey contains a whole range of other volatile constituents, some of which are also selectively lost. In many cases this seems to be beneficial to the overall product flavour.

Chapter 13
Aeneas Coffey

Andrew Coffey was employed as an engineer in Dublin city Waterworks from 1774 –1832. He had a son, Aeneas (1780 – 1852) who became an Irish excise officer in 1800. In 1810, while working in Donegal with a large body of militia, in extensive operations against the illicit Distillers, the group were ambushed near Culduff, and severely beaten. Coffey was stabbed with a bayonet and left for dead. However, he survived and the following year was promoted to the position of Excise Inspector-General. During his work with the excise he would have visited distilleries regularly. Irish pot stills are large, for example at Jameson's Bow Street distillery the wash stills each had a capacity of 16,500 Gallons (75240 Litres), these were all direct fired by means of a large furnace underneath and for each shift there was a squad of about six men who shovelled coal into the furnaces. I believe that one shift at Bow Street Distillery used eight tonnes of coal.

It is known that by that time Coffey had become very interested in the technical aspects of distilling and must have known that replacing coal with steam would be a much more efficient way to distil.

In 1824, Coffey retired from the excise and spent his time developing a new kind of distilling apparatus, and in 1830, he applied for a patent for a continuous still. The patent was granted on 5th February 1831.

The Coffey still is a continuous still in which fermented wash with an alcohol content of about 5% is continuously fed in at one point and a steady flow of spirit at about 66°, over proof (94.7% alcohol), flows out at another point designated the spirit plate. The plant is powered by a continuous flow of steam. Coffey's patent still comprises two tall columns called the 'Analyser' and the 'Rectifier' respectively, which are an arrangement of rectangular frames set one on top of the other. The bottom of each frame is a perforated plate and at alternate ends there is a system of down pipes. This causes the wash to flow across each plate before descending via the down pipes to the next lower one, where it flows in the opposite direction. The steam injected at the base of the analyser flows upwards through the perforations and bubbles through the wash, stripping the alcohol from it. The flow rates are controlled such that the upward flow of steam and vapour prevent any liquid from passing through the perforations. Spent wash emerges from the base of the analyser in a continuous flow, having virtually all of the alcohol stripped from it.

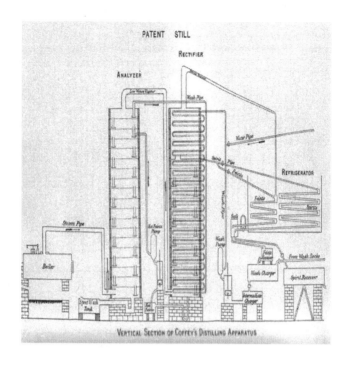

VERTICAL SECTION OF COFFEY'S DISTILLING APPARATUS

The vapour arriving at the top of the analyser is conducted through two large pipes to the bottom of the rectifier, where it flows upwards while being gradually cooled by pipes containing the incoming wash, thus, pre-heating the incoming wash. At a point near the top of the rectifier called the 'spirit bend', the final product is removed and cooled on its way to the spirit receiver. Fractions emerging from both top and bottom of the rectifier are called 'feints' and after separation of fusel oil, which is disposed of, are re-cycled into the wash feed.

Like all new developments there were initial problems, and the spirit produced had an unpleasant taste. Coffey quickly traced the problem to the use of iron in some of the pipe work and replaced the iron with copper. In the days of the malt tax, the distillers in Ireland developed a mash bill containing 40% malt, the balance being made up mainly of unmalted barley. They also developed a distillation process which produced a final spirit at about 86% by volume. Everyone agreed that this produced a spirit which tasted better and was more marketable, particularly internationally, and as such, Irish whiskey made this way became the number one whiskey in England and also made substantial inroads in America. It would seem that Coffey believed that by developing a continuous process which was heated by steam, he could push out the two previously described boundaries in the manufacture of Irish Whiskey –

- Reduce the malt content to 20%,
- increase the distillate strength to 94.8%,

These things brought about considerable cost savings in both energy and raw materials. Coffey may well have believed that he would also achieve an equivalent product improvement, however this was not so, and his product was shunned by the Irish whiskey distillers who were already successful on the English market with their pot distilled product. The Coffey still was attractive to producers of gin because it made a much purer base with which to distil the gin botanicals. And it was also used for making whiskey which was cheaper to produce, light in taste and faster maturing. In fact, some people believed that it did not require maturing.

In 1840, Coffey set up a factory in Bromley, England and the orders started flowing in. Distilleries based on the Coffey still appeared. One of the first was built by a man named Stein at a place called Kilbagie in Clackmannanshire, Scotland.

Disputes arose between the traditional distillers in Scotland and Ireland and the patent still distillers. The traditional distillers alleged that the Coffey still product was not real whisky.

Things came to a head where an outlet in Islington, London who were serving Coffey still whiskey were accused of misrepresentation. It was a case that the local courts felt unable to deal with and this led to the setting up of a Royal Commission, which reported in 1908 to adjudicate on the subject. Its findings defined whisky made in the patent still as 'Grain Whisky' and a mixture of grain whisky with malt whisky was defined as 'Blended Whisky'. Soon a number of distilleries in Scotland were set up to produce grain whisky, some of which had been converted from malt distilleries. As a result, grain whiskey, which was considerably cheaper than malt whisky, became available for blending within three years.

This brought about a number of significant changes to the Scotch Whiskey industry which still exists today, and which have, and continue to have, a significant role in the development of Scotch Whisky as it is today.

Chapter 14
Scotch Whisky

The outcome of the Royal Commission in 1908, brought about far-reaching changes in the Scotch Whisky industry. Prior to the invention of the Coffey Still, there were a large number of distilleries in Scotland using pot stills. Many on the islands and remote parts of the highlands were very small and mainly supplying their local areas. Conversely, many of the distilleries in central Scotland where the population was much larger were producing between one and two million gallons annually. Most of these gradually adopted Coffey's continuous still after it was patented in 1830. This enabled them to produce much more economically and to make a whisky with a lighter taste, which they believed the market wanted.

A number of these large grain distilleries were acquired by the Distillers Company Limited (D.C.L.), and I joined that Company as a laboratory assistant in 1955. During this time, I studied third level education on a part time basis and eventually became a research chemist. I worked in the general Laboratory located on the site of the former Glenochil Distillery, at Menstrie, near Alloa. Glenochil had originally been a malt distillery, but was converted to a grain distillery and had been closed for a number of years and was now a yeast factory.

It is interesting to note that when I arrived at Glenochil, I learned that my late grandfather Edward N. Court had been one of the excise officers there. I used to cycle about three and a half miles to work, and usually met up with some of my work mates who also lived in Alloa.

The General Laboratory carried out analytical and quality control work for the Company's five grain distilleries – Port Dundas in Glasgow, Cambus near Alloa, Carsebridge in Alloa, Cameronbridge at Windygates in Fife and Caledonian in Edinburgh; I visited all but Cameronbridge and worked at some, mainly Port Dundas and Caledonian. At the same time a number of other grain distilleries were set up in competition.

According to the findings of the Royal Commission, grain whisky has to be made from cereal – any cereal, saccharified with the enzymes of malt. Because malt is at least twice the cost of cereal it is expedient to minimise the malt percentage to the lowest value consistent with obtaining satisfactory conversion of the starch. This usually comes to about 20% malt. However, in Canada they grow six row barley as opposed to two row barley, which is normally grown in Europe. Malt made from six row barley has a higher enzyme count than its two-row equivalent and so it is possible reduce the malt percentage used. In this case it is usually 15%

The type of cereal used is not specified. Originally it was barley and then maize, either South African white maize or yellow American corn, but I have heard about grain whisky also made from wheat, rice, millet and sorghum.

When the Royal Commission defined grain whisky, it also defined malt whisky as being produced from 100% malt and distilled in pot stills. Finally it defined blended whisky as being a mixture of the two, then the whole concept of blending took root. The availability of a range of malt whiskies as well as some grain, enabled blenders to produce a blended whisky, which in their judgement, matched the taste preferences of the target market as well as limiting the malt content so as to minimise the cost. These people were not distillers themselves, but often retailers of other spirits including wines. This brought about an emphasis on marketing in the sale and export of scotch whiskies, which, moved the whole industry from production to marketing orientation. Some of the well-known whisky houses such as Johnny Walker of Kilmarnock and Dewar's of Perth, started out as wine merchants and grocers.

It also heralded to emergence of the so-called 'Whisky Barons'. They included John Baron Forteviot and Thomas Baron Dewar who developed Dewar's White Label, James Buchanan who developed Black and White, James Baron Stevenson and Sir Alexander Walker KBE, who developed Johnnie Walker, Sir Peter Mackie who developed White Horse, and Earl Haig, Dawick, Baron Haig, and Laird of Bemersyde, set up Haig & Haig.

They were all highly competitive and soon realised the Scottish and English markets could not deliver the sales volumes they required, and as a result started to develop export markets.

The blenders looked for a large range of malt whiskies to be available to them so that they could optimise their blends from the point of view of both flavour and cost.

Furthermore, whisky is a timeless product and it is essential that each brand delivers the same product year after year and, bearing in mind that some malt whiskies were matured for many more than the statutory three years, therefore, there had to be a lot of forward planning. To guarantee future supplies, the blenders preferred to buy the whisky new, to be matured preferably, under their own control. This also led to brokers and bonders who bought selected new spirits and sold on the matured equivalent.

Scotch whisky is the most widely distributed internationally. There are up to 150 malt distilleries, some of which are very small, and all using essentially the same techniques. Peat has been used in kilning the malt and a range of phenolic substances in the peat smoke is absorbed in the malt, some of which is transferred to the whisky. Malt whiskies made from a high percentage of peated malt have a distinctive taste of peat which some find attractive. The only other differences in Scottish malt whiskies are attributed to regional factors and details about still size and design.

Unique to Scotland, malt distillers sell a high proportion of their output the same day as it is distilled where it is shipped off to a blender or broker to be filled into casks and put into a warehouse to mature. As a result, only a very small proportion of the output of a malt distillery is matured by the distiller and this is usually sold as the name of the distillery and at a considerable age, usually ten, twelve or more years matured. These whiskies can present a very enjoyable drinking experience and consequently command very high prices.

This system allows new distilleries to be set up, and provided the spirit is of sufficient quality, sales can be achieved almost immediately with consequent cash flow to sustain the operation and to fund the small proportion being warehoused to be sold as an aged product in the future.

The well-known international brands of blended whisky come from large marketing-oriented companies, who buy a range of malt and grain whiskies, to be blended together with grain whisky, to produce their standard product. A typical scotch whiskey blend can contain up to 40 different malts, some of which may have been peated as well as grain whisky from two or three different grain distilleries. This system means that whiskies of different types and different ages are available from whisky brokers, and also to some extent from blenders because the available whiskies in stock are not always exactly what is required for the current blend and excesses are sold or swapped between blending houses and brokers. This system also gives rise to a number of small marketing houses. I have visited more than one, not all of which are located in Scotland who have commissioned the bottling and blending facility to put together a blend, which they have approved. It is then bottled, and labelled with the brand name and design produced by the marketing company. Some of these operations are very small and they very often concentrate on one export market. For example, I visited one which focussed exclusively on Portugal for sales. I can assume that the sales man there had good contacts in Portugal and was probably a fluent Portuguese speaker. All these activities add to the overall Scotch whisky operation giving it diversity and access to specialised markets.

Pot stills in a Scottish Malt Whisky

Chapter 15
Further Developments in
Irish Whiskey

There once were a large number of whiskey distilleries in Ireland, but the numbers gradually reduced for several reasons. First, the imposition of alcohol duty made it necessary for the authorities to aspire to having a relatively small number of large distilleries so that they could be adequately supervised. Secondly, while large distilleries were located adjacent to nearby rivers to avail of water power, the advent of steam power made it possible to build larger distilleries and to locate them in the most advantageous places. Cities were generally chosen because they provided a workforce, and those with docks provided easy access to the main export market, England.

Various distilleries fell by the wayside, for these and other reasons. And finally, the Republic of Ireland in 1950 had five operating distilleries. The main production method was the same for all five with minor variants which gave rise to notable differences in taste.

The Irish whiskey process until 1970 comprised a mash bill consisting of 40% malt, the balance made up predominantly of barley, but usually included small amounts of other cereals. At Jameson, there was 40% malt, 4% oats, and the balance made up mainly of barley but included small quantities of wheat and rye. I believe that the small quantities of wheat and rye were used to maintain the tradition, and that since the economic forces having favoured barley, no one had the courage to eliminate wheat and rye completely. The oats had another function, that in order to get adequate saccharification the barley had to be ground very finely, which meant that only the malt husks were available to form the filter bed, the oats augmented this and assisted in the drainage. All five distilleries drained from the bottom and from the side through side-lets producing wort containing a fair proportion of particulate matter.

Fermentation was achieved by the addition of distiller's yeast and brewer's yeast. No adequate reason was given for using the two but it was generally thought that the quality of the distiller's yeast at that time was unreliable and the brewer's yeast compensated for what was lacking in fermentation power. The whiskey was distilled in the traditional Irish three-stage process, in which the stills were fitted with line-arms which were cooled and the condensate returned via the so-called 'foul pipe'. The low wines were collected in strong and weak fractions. The strong fractions were used, first of all, to produce strong feints at a strength of 76% alcohol by volume. Various quantities of strong low wines were combined with strong feints and used to distil the final product. Weak low wines were distilled along with recycled weak feints in the feints still producing a quantity of strong feints and further weak feints. It can be seen that, apart from the small quantity of strong low wines added to the strong feints, the new whiskey was distilled from spirits which had been distilled not only three times, but many segments of them for much more than that. The low wines produced had a total volume of 27.5% of the original wash, which is consistent with a reflux level in the spirit still of about 25%. Stills were direct-fired with coal, they also contained small internal steam coils from which the contribution towards heating was minimal.

The contents of the stills were agitated using a mechanical mixer. The new whiskey was filled into oak casks at an alcoholic strength of 25° over proof, just over 71% by volume. The legal maturation time in Ireland was then five years, and it was the practice to mature spirits for much longer. John Jameson had a slogan 'not a drop is sold till its seven years old'.

Much of the whiskey was sold new to bonders, who matured the whiskey and bottled under the distiller's name. The distillers normally supplied the labels, but even then, the packaging standards were generally inferior. During the 50s and 60s, there was a move towards bringing bottling and marketing into the control of the distiller. And this was accompanied by better and more up-to-date standards of presentation and packaging. During the 1950s, both Lockes of Kilbeggan and Williams of Tullamore fell by the wayside and the Tullamore Dew brand was acquired by Powers as a potential Powers export brand.

Apart from the advance in Scotch, Irish whiskey was challenged by a whole series of problems – beginning with political unrest in Ireland and the First World War, then prohibition in the United States from 1920 – 1933. The American market was particularly important for Irish whiskey because an estimated 40 million Americans claim to have Irish origins, and the country has a great love for Ireland and its people. Early immigration from Ireland found people struggling to survive in the new world, and if they drank whisky at all, it was more likely to have been cheaper locally produced rye or bourbon whiskey.

The end of World War Two brought about developments in the Irish drinks Industry. Cork distilleries started to produce Cork Dry Gin, which found substantial success among Irish consumers albeit protected by a tariff on imported spirits. This protection disappeared in the late 60s by the signing of the Anglo-Irish trade agreement. At this time Cork Dry Gin enjoyed greater than 80% of the Irish Gin market. Powers Gin around that time also appeared but the product did not make any substantial headway. Vodka also emerged as a new white spirit. Smirnoff was made in Ireland by Gilbeys, Saratov was made by Powers and Nordoff was made by Cork Distilleries Company, neither of these two products matched the standard of Smirnoff and this was reflected in sales.

At the end of World War II, transatlantic air travel began. There were no modern style airports so flying boats were used. The West of Ireland is the closest point to the United States and was therefore, targeted as the best place to land. Fortunately, the Shannon Estuary provides a large area of relatively calm water suitable for this and the terminal was based in a small town called Foynes, near Limerick. Flying boats are piston engine and propeller driven and as such fly at a maximum speed of about 300 mph, unlike a modern jet airliner which can travel at twice that speed. This means that a transatlantic flight by flying boat would take at least 12 hours, and even more allowing for the necessary refuelling stops at Iceland or the Azores. Aircraft of this type are noisy and have a lot of vibration, and so the comfort level is relatively low. Nevertheless, many people found it preferable to travelling by ship, taking a week or more.

When the flying boats landed at Foynes, the passengers had to disembark into a small boat to be taken ashore, they were no doubt very tired by this stage and exhausted by their travels. The head chef at Foynes was a man called Joe Sheridan and he was charged with offering the visitors food and drink, which they would find memorable and provide a satisfactory welcome to Ireland. Sheridan was instructed that everything on the menu had to be Irish, however, he knew that the first thing Americans would want when coming ashore was coffee. Everybody knows that coffee beans will not grow in the Irish climate, and so the challenge was to add a number of things to the coffee so that it could be called Irish. The obvious addition was Irish whiskey, sugar, and of course cream, for which Ireland is known for its quality and richness. Finally, Sheridan served his coffee in a stemmed glass, so that it could be held by the stem, and he floated the cream on the top of a dark coffee to mimic the appearance of the internationally known Irish stout. Thus, it could be called Irish Coffee. From then on, the whiskey distillers saw this as an opportunity to sell their whiskey overseas, particularly in the United States. It was known at that stage that Irish whiskey was not a preferred taste in the U.S. because it had a bitter aftertaste, which was disliked and unfortunately emphasized by the presence of ice, which was normal in America. These aspects of Irish whiskey were being worked on by the research team in the late 60s but in the meantime it

111

was important to sell whiskey and to maintain continuity in the U.S. market. Irish coffee was seen as a potential route to achieve this.

The former chairman of John Jameson told a story of a situation in the U.S. when he was trying to introduce the concept of Irish coffee. He was talking to a group of American sales and marketing executives, and was told that they didn't want coffee because it would keep them awake, they didn't want Irish whiskey because they didn't like Irish whiskey, they didn't want sugar because it was fattening and they didn't want cream because they were trying to control their cholesterol intake. But each of them drank an Irish coffee, and when they were finished, they had another one. A friend of mine in Canada had an old uncle who was a retired bishop, who was exceedingly difficult to entertain. When the bishop came to spend a few days with him and his wife, they were not particularly looking forward to the occasion, except the saving grace was that the bishop usually went to bed very early. However, on his first day he was served an Irish coffee, then he had a second one and finally challenged them to a game of bridge which continued until 3 am.

A bar in Fisherman's Wharf in San Francisco introduced Irish coffee and set up an assembly line which demonstrated the product being put together and also enabled large quantities to be produced within a short time. It then became fashionable for people on their way out to the theatre, to concerts or to dinner to stop by Fisherman's Wharf for Irish coffee. This particular bar owner became a millionaire as a result of this. All of these activities provided continuity of sales and awareness for Irish whiskey.

At this time there were five Irish whiskey distilleries in production in the republic of Ireland, Cork Distilleries Co., Jameson, Powers, Williams of Tullamore and Lockes of Kilbeggan. These latter two soon ceased production and the Tullamore Dew brand was acquired by Powers which they intended to use as an export brand.

Cork Distilleries had the brand 'Paddy' made at their Midleton Distillery; they also had Watercourse Distillery which was also a yeast factory. The process they used for yeast was unable to create an entirely aerobic atmosphere, and so a quantity of alcohol was produced in the yeast propagation process. To recover this alcohol, they acquired a column still and produced neutral spirits to be used as a base for gin. Later at Watercourse Distillery, they also produced some grain whiskey. Paddy Whiskey was bottled at their North Mall bottling plant, where Cork Dry Gin was also produced. Paddy whiskey was very popular in the Munster area but had limited export potential. During the '50s and '60s, Cork Dry Gin in a square bottle with a red and white label became very popular in all of the Republic, and at one stage commanded in excess of 86% of the Irish gin market. This was hugely beneficial to the company because gin does not require maturation, and can be produced at very little cost. At Powers they developed the 'baby Power' – a miniature sized bottle which was very popular. One reported usage was that the man who had spent the evening drinking at the pub brought two baby Powers home with him so that he and his wife could have a final drink together. Powers also moved largely away from bonders and set up their own bottling plant. First of all in Drury Street, and later on, in a larger and more modern facility off the Naas Road at an area call Fox & Geese, which remains today as the main bottling plant of Irish Distillers. Powers also developed a gin which was relatively unsuccessful and together with Cork Distilleries, produced their own brands of vodka, Saratov and Nordoff.

Meanwhile Jameson had plans to develop gin and vodka, which never materialised due to other developments. Jameson had a problem related to the bonders. These were groups of companies who bought whiskey in bulk, either new or matured, and proceeded to bottle and distribute it. This was generally sold under the Jameson name and, in fact, Jameson supplied many of them with labels. These included Gilbeys, who produced 'Red Breast' and Mitchells who produced 'Green Spot'. These two latter companies were highly professional in their bottling operations and marketed high quality products. But some of the other bonders were much less professional, leading to a fair amount of inferior product being distributed. The Jameson aim was to eliminate the bonders with the exception of Gilbeys and Mitchells and to take control of their own bottling and marketing. The big problem was like the other Irish distillers; Jameson was heavily dependent on domestic market sales and dared not take any steps which would put these in jeopardy.

The first move was to develop their own ten-year-old brand, which had the Jameson Crest on the label and was called 'Crested Ten'. The brand was very successful but there was insufficient stock of upcoming ten-year-old whiskeys to depend entirely on that brand. It was necessary to develop a further brand of whiskey with no age statement on the label, and so developed the brand name 'Red Seal' with the assurance that it had been sealed at the distillery which was therefore a guarantee of quality. This began gradually to eat in to the bonder's share of the sales.

During the '60s, the English brewery mergers took place where large numbers of local breweries combined to form about five large brewery groups who controlled the English beer and pub market. One such group, Bass Charington, acquired Bushmills distillery in Northern Ireland. This raised the question as to whether the Irish Whiskey Distillers were liable to be purchased by an external enterprise, a particular fear was expressed that Cork Distilleries would be taken over because of the great success of Cork Dry Gin. To stave off this threat the three remaining Irish whiskey companies formed a merger in 1966, the group was first of all called United Distillers of Ireland, but when the initials UDI became political due to developments in what was then Rhodesia, the company was quickly changed to Irish Distillers LTD.

The formation of Irish Distillers brought about huge changes to the industry. The three founding members, instead of competing with one another on the Irish market, united to tackle export markets, particularly the United States. Kevin McCourt, the newly appointed group managing director negotiated with the Irish whiskey bonders and from then on, all sales were in bottle which had been filled and packaged in either of the company's two bottling plants, one in Cork and one in Dublin.

Marketing was reorganised, arising from the appointment of Archie Cook as marketing director and research and development aimed at improving production methods and at the same time developing new products which could be expected to yield returns faster than those gained by whiskey growth. As far as new production methods were concerned, all aspects including milling, brewing, fermentation, distillation and maturation were studied individually by technical personnel from the three original companies working together. To give one example, all the traditional distilleries drained their mash tuns from the bottom, until the bed of grains became clogged by which point they opened up side-lets allowing wort to be drawn from the top of the mash. This led to a wort containing a considerable level of particulate matter. It was agreed that a better product would result if the wort was clear, and a part of the research programme was to devise ways to obtain this result. This was helped by the use of a German style *lauter tun* which had the capability of gently raking the bed of grains so that it continued to act as a filter. The development in distillation was largely achieved by the *hybrid still* which was proven to distil a cleaner, better tasting whiskey and greatly to improve economics in the form of energy.

The important part that casks play in the taste of a whiskey is sometimes not appreciated. It had been the practice that the Spanish sherry producers exported their products in casks which, once they had been emptied and the sherry bottled, were available to be sold on to distillers. This option was closed off during the 1950s when the Spanish government decreed that sherry could only be exported in bottle. By this time, prohibition in the United States had ended and the regulation there that casks could be used only once for maturing bourbon, meant that the focus for cask supply changed from Spain to the United States. Today, freshly emptied bourbon casks are used as well as sherry butts, specially produced in Spain, which have contained Olorosso sherry for a number of months. A combination of both of these appears to optimise the taste of the whiskey.

All of the above items were addressed and built into the new group distillery located at Midleton in county Cork, using water from the Dungourney River. The New Midleton distillery had the capability to replicate all three main Irish whiskey brands to the extent that they were accepted by the public. Midleton also produced high quality grain neutral spirits for the production of gin and vodka.

When Irish Distillers was formed, a long-term plan for Irish whiskey was set up. It was recognised that this would take a fairly long lead time, which there was an investment phase to be funded. Whilst Irish coffee played its part in keeping Irish whiskey alive, it was decided that new products should be developed which would expand the sales potential and the overall performance of the company. At the formation of Irish Distillers, Cork Dry Gin was very successful. There were also two vodkas which did not appear to compete sufficiently with Irish Smirnoff made by Gilbeys. One of the first tasks was to develop a new vodka using greatly improved technology and called 'Huzzar'.

At about this time the Anglo-Irish Trade Agreement was enacted which eliminated the hitherto import tariff on Scotch whisky, making Scotch cheaper than Irish whiskey on the Irish market. For this reason, some Scotch-like versions of Irish whiskey were developed and sold at a competitive price.

In the United States, a product called Southern Comfort was developed and became very popular. It was largely assumed to be a type of whiskey, which it was not. It was made from neutral alcohol, sugar and flavourings but it was coloured and packaged like whiskey and had whiskey-like flavourings. In Irish Distillers, it was decided to follow this route by the development of a product called Mulligan. It contained a certain percentage of whiskey but also neutral spirits, flavourings and sugar and remains on the Irish market in a small way.

During the 1970s, international liquor company IDV developed a cream liqueur, a mixture of alcohol and cream which no one at that time thought would be possible. However, there are techniques which IDV gradually acquired and the product was launched as Bailey's Irish Cream. There was something about the softness and smoothness of the cream which balanced against the strong bite burn of the whiskey. When it was seen that it could be done, Irish Distillers developed a similar product called Waterford Cream, which was reasonably successful for a number of years.

Another development was West Coast Cooler, which capitalised on the great success of cooler type drinks and which is still on the market.

Once Irish Distillers was set up and operating as a group, it was decided to include Bushmills Distillery, located in Northern Ireland, within the group. A deal was made with the distillers Seagrams to acquire a share in the Irish Distiller's group yielding funds, which were then used to purchase Bushmills. The agreement with Seagrams limited their share-holding in Irish Distillers to 25% and it remained so for a number of years. Eventually, Seagrams sought to increase their share and, after several requests, when this was declined Seagrams decided to sell out, leaving Irish

Distillers in a very precarious position. Eventually, the French company Pernod Ricard bought the company and owns it to this day.

There were a number of advantages in this move, particularly that Pernod has a large, virtually worldwide, export organisation through which Irish whiskies were then able to flow. This is shown up particularly in the case of Jameson which has grown at unprecedented rates, exceeding the 6,000,000 cases per annum, and projected to go much further. Irish whiskey is coming back to being an important world brand.

Chapter 16
The Jameson Distillery

John Jameson was born in Alloa, Clackmannanshire (my hometown) on the 5th of October 1740. By 1780, he had become a Senior Administrative Officer in Clackmannan County Council, and had married Margaret Haig from the Scottish distilling family of Markinch in Fife. In that year, John, with his two sons, John and Andrew, sailed to Dublin and acquired an interest in the Bow St. distillery. He then returned home, leaving his two sons in charge of the investment. Some years later, the Jameson family became owners of that distillery.

Portrait of John Jameson by Raeburn

In the years that followed, a large number of distilleries were founded in the Dublin area, and sales of Irish whiskey in England, Irelands biggest and nearest neighbour, began to grow. Hitherto, the English, other than beer which they produced locally, drank Claret and French brandy. Over the years, Irish whiskey was gradually overtaking brandy until in 1855 the parasitic disease *Phylloxera* devastated the French vineyards. There was hardly enough wine then for the French themselves to drink, and none left over to distil into brandy, and so Brandy became unavailable on the English market and was replaced by Irish whiskey. This caused a huge boost in whiskey sales and till 1914 Irish whiskey sales in England exceeded that of scotch and brandy. Thereafter, the impact of Coffey's patented still became apparent and the whole Scotch whisky industry became market oriented.

In 1965, I was invited to join John Jameson & Sons. When I arrived at Bow Street to start work on December 13th 1965, I discovered a process vastly different from anything I had experienced in both Malt and grain whisky production. To begin with, the raw barley was not cooked as it would have been in Scotland, it was simply dried to a moisture content of 5.5% and very finely ground. The brewing process was very complicated and seemed to have been some variation on the German decoction process. The wort was cooled in the 'Morton's improved Patent Refrigerator', and the wash backs holding 33,000 gallons each were made of timber, which had been lined with sheet aluminium. The work with aluminium was obviously a fairly recent development made possible by the development of a method for welding aluminium.

There were four pot stills, two wash stills, containing 16,500 gallons each, a spirit still containing 8,000 gallons and a smaller feint still.

Aleck Crichton was a direct descendant of John Jameson. He participated in World War 2, in which he was wounded in the leg. He also played a part in the post-war occupation of West Germany. After leaving the army he returned to Bow Street Distillery to learn about distilling and to try to regenerate the fortunes of Irish whiskey and became company chairman. At that time, Jameson whiskey was sold via bonders, who matured and bottled the whiskey and unfortunately, did not always do that with the necessary degree of professionalism. The initial plan was to start bottling their own whiskey in-house, and to break into this concept, Aleck planned a premium Irish whiskey called 'Crested Ten'. As the name suggests, it was a ten years old. The bottle shape was modified to have a slightly brandy-like appearance – wide at the shoulders and with a straight neck. Considerable care was taken with the selection and preparation of the whiskey for bottling, and the product was accepted by the Irish drinkers to such an extent, that there was not sufficient whiskey available to supply; the product had to be placed on quota at times. Aleck recognised that the plant and process at Bow Street was mostly over 100 years old, and that a degree of modernisation was necessary if this product was going to compete internationally.

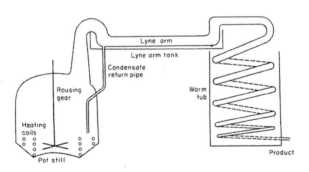

This is a drawing of a typical Irish pot still, the neck is located at the side to accommodate a vertical shaft for the rousing gear, and in my view the neck is too narrow causing a relatively high vapour velocity in the neck leading to dangers of entrainment. I would have chosen a centrally located neck, of much wider diameter and made alternative arrangements for the stirring gear if such was necessary.

This diagram shows heating coils which were installed at Bow Street later, but initially each still was fired with a central furnace and the hot gases circulating around the flue plates. The line arm, as you can see, is immersed in a tank of cold water with a foul pipe which returns condensate to the liquid in the still. The condenser comprises a copper worm of diminishing diameter, immersed in a large tank of cold water. The worm tub of the second wash still was filled, not with cold water, but with the next charge of wash as a result of which the wash was pre-heated somewhat and that resulted in some energy efficiency.

The two basic tasks I was given was first, to find a better way of making the whiskey and also to make better whiskey.

On the former, I quickly noted that the methods used required an excessively large work force, and my initial plan was to introduce a degree of mechanisation with a view to substantially reducing operating costs. The stills were coal fired, and although I never obtained an accurate account of the costs, I am quite certain that it would have been much greater than the obvious alternative of steam heating. Furthermore, it involved a squad of five men working on a three-shift system, shovelling the coal into the furnaces under the stills. Steam heating was one obvious cost-saving exercise, saving both energy and labour. But it was not the significant issue which I tackled first. In the mills, the cereal was ground and the grist was collected in sacks, placed on weighing scales, and carefully measured so that each sack contained one barrel, a weight equal to 168 lbs or 76.4 kgs. The sacks were wheeled from the mill room to the mash loft where they were assembled neatly in rows, and it was one of my first jobs as an assistant distiller to count the sacks of barley, malt, oats, wheat and rye and confirm that the numbers conformed to the long-established recipe. When this was complete, I gave authority to mash at which point the operatives emptied the contents of the sacks through four chutes from the floor of the mash loft to the mash tun or kieve. The kieve contained a quantity of water at approximately 120° Fahrenheit, and starting with the malt the cereals, were dropped down into the water where the stirring gear mixed it. During this time, hotter liquor was added to the kieve until the mashing was complete. The temperature had to be checked and confirmed by the distiller in charge to 144°F (62.5°C). The mash was allowed to settle and then drainage began through the underlets. After some time, the side lets were opened so the mash was drained from both top and bottom leading to a fairly high proportion of particulate matter in the wort. On my recommendation, the company invested in grist cases automatic weighers and some conveyers so that the grist was automatically weighed into the grist cases and then conveyed into the keives at mashing in time. This development produced a reduction in the workforce of 17 as well as substantial saving in operating cost, which rapidly financed the capital costs.

It has already been mentioned that the wort was cooled using a Morton's refrigerator, but such an arrangement did not allow for recovering heat from the wort for subsequent re-use. On my advice, the company purchased an Alfa Laval plate heat exchanger in which the heat was extracted from cooling the wort-heated water which was used for the subsequent mash, thereby providing an element of heat recovery. Converting the stills to steam heating brought another series of problems. The oil-fired boilers, that had been modernised in 1919, were rated at 10,000 lbs of steam per hour, and there were three of them, giving 30,000 lbs per hour. But there were doubts given the age of the boilers as to whether they were still capable of delivering their full potential. The theoretical calculation of the steam requirement came to 24,000 lbs per hour, and an allowance for losses etc. brought the value up to 27,000 per hour. The steam pipe going to the boiler house was not big enough (four inches), to transmit the necessary quantity of steam efficiently and for this reason a new pipeline of an eight-inch diameter was installed. There were further problems due to condensate return, which were ultimately solved by installing a simple ball cock in the condensate tank. We were finally able to operate the distillery entirely on steam with a saving of at least 15 jobs and an undoubted reduction in energy costs. At that stage, the energy consumption was equivalent to 33.61 mega joules per litre of pure alcohol that is at least 10% higher than the most efficient Scottish malt distilleries.

To address the question of product quality, there were a number of points to be considered. The clear target was to produce a whiskey which would stand up internationally against the big brands of Scotch, Canadian and American whiskeys. It was thought that to do this, the product would be so far removed in taste from that being currently sold on the Irish market, and that there was a danger in losing market share on the domestic market which would have disastrous consequences for the company. Finally, we did end up having a special North American formula for a short time, this was achieved by blending with grain whiskey to lighten the overall product taste. But it was proved that if the flavour of the main product moved gradually in a positive direction, acceptance by the traditional drinkers would remain static or even perhaps improve. The main points discussed were the fact that there was a bitter element in the taste, which was greatly emphasised by the addition of ice. And although it was not the practice back home in Ireland to add ice to whiskey, it was certainly normal practice in the United States. This bitterness was otherwise defined as a 'shudder', the reaction to the first taste of whiskey as it was then. A new way of distilling to eliminate these elements had to be pursued. We built a laboratory distillation plant in which a number of experimental distillations were made and from which we concluded a number of points.

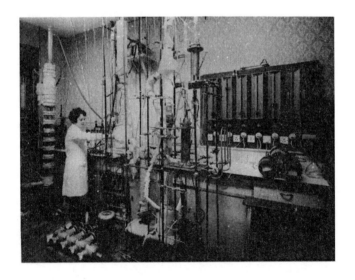

It appeared that distillation achieves three objectives

1. To extract substantially all of the alcohol as well as other volatile materials arising from the raw material

and from the fermentation process into a clear alcoholic liquid which we call low wines.

2. To redistill portions of low wines together with recycled fractions from previous distillations, to make a mixture of feints at 76% alcohol by volume which can be distilled into a final product.

3. To recover alcohol from the weak fractions.

This third process is done mainly using the feints still which throughout its distillation is operating at a low alcoholic strength, and therefore, is uneconomic. Furthermore, tastings of the so produced strong and the weak feints revealed that the unpleasant bitter notes identified in the final product were present; and indeed these fractions may in fact be the only source of these unpleasant elements.

A pot still is a relatively inefficient instrument for distilling alcohol, but is also essential if the final product is to be whiskey. Conversely, a column still, such as the update of Coffey's design, is a much more economical way of recovering the alcohol in a purer clearer form and mainly or wholly free from some of the bitter elements previously identified. A column still is also a much more economical way of distilling alcohol.

As a result of these considerations, we devised a modified technique for distilling Irish whiskey where a column still was introduced purely to recover alcohol from the weak fractions which resulted in a much cleaner final product, with the clearly identifiable traditional character but lacking in some of the unpleasant bitter notes previously identified. Not only did this process greatly enhance the final product's flavour, but it reduced the distillation energy requirement from 33.61–19.21 mega joules per litre of pure alcohol.

This product was called 'modified pot still whiskey' later reduced to 'mod-pot'.

BOW STREET DISTILLERY, DUBLIN.

The John Jameson Distillery in the late 19th Century

Presentation and Design

Following the successful launch of the Crested Ten as a premium, it was imperative to move into the general range represented by the Jameson seven-year-old, but it was also important to follow the lead of Crested Ten and to get over the message that it was distillery-bottled. This was all carried out on the initiative of Aleck Crichton who kindly involved me in some of the discussions. A number of decisions were made. The brand was called Red Seal, and it was decided not to have an 'age' statement on the bottle. A label was designed and I persuaded the company to adopt a green bottle for this product. I convinced them by making out a list of a large number of internationally successful drinks, which were packed in bottles made of green glass. One difficulty was that the Irish glass bottle company did not have the capability of producing green glass. The main thrust of their business was to produce amber-coloured Guinness bottles, so eventually the company went to German bottle manufacturer Gerresheimer Glas, who produced a consignment of excellent quality green bottles (subsequently the Irish glass bottle company very quickly learned how to make bottles with green glass). A new set of labels was designed to give a quite excellent pack where eventually the Red Seal name was abandoned and the product became simply 'Jameson'.

John Jameson Irish Whiskey

The success of Irish coffee prompted Jameson to develop Irish Velvet. It was a sort of instant Irish coffee where the coffee, sugar and whiskey were all combined in the bottle to give a syrupy liquid. A measure of this, when poured into a glass and topped up with hot water produced an excellent Irish coffee which only required to be topped off with cream. This topping off process was made much easier because the Irish Velvet was designed with a high specific gravity making it easier for the cream to float. This was frequently a problem with the traditional Irish coffee where, generally too much whiskey had been added thereby lowering the specific gravity, causing the cream to sink or mix up with the coffee, departing from the traditional appearance to the detriment of the entire effect.

Chapter 17
Quality Control

Any manufacturer producing a product for human consumption must ensure against offering defective product for sale. When checking out whiskey, it is clearly necessary to approach the product in the same manner as the intended consumer. A consumer would first of all be influenced by the appearance of the product and then by the aroma and finally the taste. In the case of whiskey, much of the product imagery is portrayed by the packaging which must also be consistent.

Whiskey is normally a beautiful amber colour and it should be clear because a cloudy product is much less appealing to the consumer. The taste of the product must be assessed at various stages in the production and it is the responsibility of the producer to supply a product which is consistent from batch to batch. This calls for a degree of testing, of which there are two main routes, either tasting or analysis.

When considering this, I would cite the following example – imagine a room full of people with an air analyser set up, constantly analysing the air in the room and printing out the analysis every 15 seconds. Suddenly, a lady enters the room wearing perfume. Virtually everyone in the room immediately recognises that someone wearing perfume has entered the room and indeed some people may even be able to identify the brand of perfume. The question is what does the air analyser show? And the answer is absolutely nothing. It does not detect any difference in the air quality in the room before and after the arrival of the perfume aroma.

The moral of the story is that the human nose is much more sensitive than any machine, however sophisticated, even in newer versions which have become much more sensitive, and so the nose should be used as the final arbiter when it comes to product aroma and taste. It is interesting to note that dogs have an even more powerful sense of smell, but unless and until someone works out a technique whereby a dog can communicate its thoughts, I suppose we must make do with the human nose. The human nose contains a vast number of odour receptors and is believed to be able to recognise up to five thousand different aromas.

Whiskey should be tasted in a stemmed glass; the reason for this is that by holding the base you can keep your hands as far away as possible from the point where you are nosing. Depending on what you have been doing, and that is your own business, but to give two examples, you might just have washed your hands where they have an aroma from soap or gel, or alternatively you might just have fuelled your car where there may be residual petroleum on your hands. So the secret is to keep your hands as far away as possible from the top of the glass. The glasses should be small, and preferably narrow at the top to concentrate the vapours.

It is essential that samples being compared are all at the same alcoholic strength and temperature. My preference is

20% by volume, which means that whiskey at bottling strength must be diluted 50/50 by, preferably, purified, water. Whiskey samples taken earlier in the process at higher alcoholic strengths would require more water to bring their strength down to 20%. Most routine production testing is one of comparison where a sample of satisfactory product exists and the new batch can be compared to ensure that it meets that standard.

This is best done using the triangular test, where three glasses are filled – one or two with the sample under test and one or two of the standard and therefore unknown to the taster that there are two samples identical and a third one which may or may not be different. The challenge to the taster is identifying the odd one out. If they can, that indicates there is some degree of difference. If they cannot successfully select the odd one, that is proof that there is no difference between the samples and that the sample under test conforms fully with the standard.

I have used the word tasting, but it is my advice that very little tasting be done because the palate can very quickly lose its sensitivity. It is my recommendation that all early assessment is done by nosing, and that tasting should be restricted to making a final confirmation of the assessment.

On the question of analysis, most companies choose to use both taste testing and analysis to check out their final product; if both of these tests give satisfactory results, then you can be fairly confident that the product is within specification. In the event that there are some doubts about this, the analysis compared with a database of all previous analyses may provide some clues as to the possible reasons for the off-specification result and may indeed point to a way for solving that particular difficulty. Generally speaking, analysis results for each component should come within one standard deviation of those in the database, but variations of greater than one standard deviation or perhaps as high as two standard deviations are an indication that something is amiss requiring serious attention.

With regard to appearance, whiskey as it emerges from the still is brilliantly clear, however it contains a number of alcohol-soluble esters which diminish in solubility with diminishing alcoholic strength, and although the whiskey is brilliantly clear when it emerges from the cask, at around 60% alcohol, it tends to form a cloud when the strength is reduced to bottling strength of 40% alcohol. For this reason it is normal to filter whiskey prior to bottling, but allowance must be made for the fact that some of the complex changes which bring about the cloud are not instantaneous and may take a certain time to form. This could be 24 hours or more and is temperature dependant. Whiskey which has been filtered clear may continue to produce a cloud if the filtration was carried out too soon. To overcome some of these problems, it is usual to filter at a reduced temperature. For example, the whiskey should always be filtered at a temperature lower than that which is likely to be consumed.

Some distillers, by using very low temperatures, can foreshorten the necessary settling down time, but it is worth bearing in mind that the lower the temperature at the point of filtration, the more different flavouring materials are eliminated from the final product, with a loss of the overall character and complexity. Temperatures for filtration between -3 ^{0}C and -10 ^{0}C are common. Some connoisseurs prefer the full, unfiltered flavour and are prepared either to tolerate a slight cloud or to buy a whiskey bottle at higher strength. Whatever you plan to do, there can still be pitfalls as illustrated by the following account.

Some years ago, when working for Irish Distillers, I flew from Dublin to Frankfurt in Germany and met with my colleague, David Greer, who was a regional export director. We dined together in Frankfurt and the next day travelled by train to Wiesbaden, which is situated on the River Rhine, and famous in former times for its hot springs.

We went to visit Henkell & Co., famous for its sparkling wine *Henkell Trocken* which could be described as German champagne. We entered the magnificent Henkell head office, to be met by Adolf von Ribbentrop, son of the famous Jaochim von Ribbentrop, who was a member of the Nazi Party and was German Foreign Minister from 1939 until he was found guilty of war crimes at Nuremberg in 1945 and executed by hanging. Adolf was called after his even more famous Godfather, Adolf Hitler.

We entered a beautiful hall with square-shaped pillars and a double staircase at the far end. Between the pillars there were small tables and chairs where we were invited to sit down and offered a glass of Henkell Trocken.

We found Adolf to be a most charming and courteous man who was tall and well-groomed and spoke perfect English. His mother was Anna Henkell of the long-established wine producing family, and in peacetime, Adolf was working for that company. He indicated that they had a problem with a consignment of our whiskey and we were invited to go with him to the warehouse to examine the problem. As soon as I saw the bottles, I knew immediately what was wrong; as quality controller it was my job to deal with the problem, and at this stage my job was easy. I ordered that the consignment be returned to Ireland and replaced. David took care of the details and Adolf was happy with the outcome of his complaint. I was then able to fly home, at which point my job became much more difficult. I knew what was wrong but I had to find out why it went wrong and, more importantly, what procedures should be put in place to avoid a recurrence.

The substance I saw at the bottom of the bottles in Wiesbaden was like a small group of tiny white flower petals. It was calcium oxalate, produced by the combination of oxalic acid and calcium. Neither of these substances is a natural constituent of whiskey, so how did this happen?

Irish whiskey is matured in used casks, some which previously contained various types of wine, and some wines do contain small amounts of oxalic acid. Calcium is a natural constituent of water and is largely responsible for what we call hardness. If we cannot be sure that oxalate is absent from the whiskey, we must be sure that no calcium is added as part of reducing water.

But, I hear you ask, if the whiskey has been filtered clear at the time of bottling, where did the flower petals of oxalate come from? The fact is that the oxalate reaction is very slow, taking days and weeks to form, and so the whiskey was apparently perfect when it left Ireland but there was oxalic acid and calcium lurking in it. Over the following weeks, the little white crystals slowly formed.

This would not have affected the taste or any other aspect of the whiskey, but when you sell something like whiskey, it must be perfect.

For the above reasons, the water used to reduce whiskey must be purified such that all-natural minerals, including calcium, are removed, and I later discovered that a breakdown in the water purification plant caused the problem. Strict instructions were issued by the management to insure that this problem would not recur.

Presentation is particularly important, bearing in mind that more people will see your pack on the shelf of an outlet than will actually taste the product, and so early impressions of the care with which the product has been presented may contribute towards persuading the intending customer to purchase. It is not simply a question that your bottle leaves the production unit in excellent condition, but it has to endure the rigours of transportation so that the same excellent condition is visible when the bottle appears on the shelf. To address this situation, Irish Distillers arranged to have a number of bottles of their product purchased anonymously in various randomly selected parts of the United States. These were carefully wrapped and returned to Ireland such that the condition of the bottle on the shelf could be assessed and could be compared with the condition ex-factory.

Label scuffing was one issue because, strangely enough, a bottle contained in a cardboard cell in a carton rotates as a result of vibration during transportation. This problem was overcome by working with the glass producers and arranging such things as an 'eyebrow' where a small ridge of glass avoided contact between the label and the cardboard surface within the carton. Other techniques including tapering of the bottle or situating the label within a panel, were also devised. Likewise, label manufacturers who also took the problem seriously devised various tough varnishes to produce labels which were resistant to scuffing.

The closure was another area. Many of the ROPP (roll on pilfer proof) designs of screw caps could not be turned or spun around without engaging sufficiently in the threads and either way could not be removed. A more functional closure was required and, the industry generally moved to stelcaps; they were functionally better than ROPPs and aesthetically more pleasing. Premium whiskies today tend to have a cork and capsule closure, but when the use of lead in the manufacture of capsules became illegal, the tin capsules which replaced them were found to be much more difficult to remove.

It is clear that manufacturers of bottles, labels and closures, production people involved in bottling and handling and marketing personal involved in design and aesthetics must work together to produce a consistent product which would be sufficiently durable to arrive on the retail shelf in good condition.

Chapter 18
Climate Change

There are a number of serious problems relating to the condition and viability of the planet. Items like plastic in the oceans, land fill, recycling, overproduction of certain items, overwhelming amounts of waste etc. This is not about these, important as they are. This is about energy.

A recent BBC television documentary presented by Sir David Attenborough on the subject, gives some startling evidence of the importance of just small increases in average global temperatures. The situation is deteriorating rapidly and some predict that in a few short years, the planet will be unable to support life as we know it.

This global temperature-increase is attributed to the sudden rise of carbon dioxide in the atmosphere. In the year 1800, the level was 280 parts per million, but since then it has risen to its 2017 level of 405 parts per million and continues to increase at an alarming rate.

The carbon dioxide together with smaller quantities of other gases like methane collect in the upper atmosphere and form a barrier which allows heat in the form of solar radiation to pass through but stops heat flow in the opposite direction (Sometimes called the greenhouse effect).

When vegetation began to grow in the early days of the planet, plants, as they do today, absorbed carbon dioxide from the atmosphere. This was processed within the leaves, in the presence of water and sunlight, to form two types of sugar. One type, based on glucose, supplied the energy to fuel the plant growth, and the other, based on cellobiose, provided the building blocks of roots, stems and leaves etc. Many plants have a life of just one year, and most others have a life of only a few years. When they die they release their carbon dioxide directly back to the atmosphere. This gives a steady balanced level of carbon dioxide of about 200 parts per million.

Not all plants release their carbon dioxide back into the atmosphere. One example is trees. Most trees live anything from 10 to 100 years and some live a great deal longer. Before there was any human involvement, dead trees would fall down and slowly begin to rot. It was at a time when the planet was prone to very unsettled conditions. There were earth quakes, landslides and other disturbances. Frequently, groups of these fallen trees would become buried under the earth. Depending on the conditions, the rotting process took different forms leading to different final products. These are coal, oil or natural gas, or on vary rare occasions the coal would crystallise out as diamonds.

Probably around the twelfth century, and I believe this happened in Belgium, it was reported that stones dug up from the ground would burn and give off good heat. The practice spread and soon coal was being dug up and burned at numerous locations worldwide. By burning coal and other fossil fuels, carbon dioxide, which had been taken from the atmosphere many centuries or even millennia ago, was released into the atmosphere, in addition to the carbon dioxide from plants grown during the previous few years. The industrial revolution and the invention of the motor vehicles all accelerated the demand for the fossil fuels. Carbon dioxide which is released to the atmosphere within a few years of being absorbed can be termed 'carbon neutral'. One example would be the carbon dioxide which bubbles off a fermentation in a brewery or distillery.

Global warming, as its name suggests, is a global matter and must be addressed on a worldwide scale. Whiskey distilleries are somewhat energy intensive. About 85-90% of the energy is thermal and normally produced, either directly or by raising steam using one or more fossil fuels. We have calculated that a typical highly efficient small Irish whiskey distillery would emit 12,000 tonnes of carbon dioxide in a year. If what is otherwise an excellent future for Irish whiskey is to be achieved, it is important to find ways to eliminate carbon dioxide emissions from fossil fuels.

In a process called anaerobic digestion, the waste materials, including the spent grains from a distillery, can be processed to produce the gas methane. This is almost identical to natural gas but since it was derived from the carbon dioxide absorbed by the cereals during the previous season, it can be regarded as carbon neutral. To date, by using as many energy saving techniques as possible, during the design process it is possible to generate sufficient methane to provide a high proportion of the total thermal energy requirement of the distillery. If we are to improve upon this, it is necessary to find ways of further reducing the thermal energy requirement. This can be approached in a number of ways, either by finding ways to increase the output of ethane from the A.D. plant possibly by sourcing additional bio degradable feed material, or by reducing the energy requirement of the distillery.

Virtually all whiskeys depend to some degree on the pot still. In a pot still the alcohol content within the pot gradually diminishes to a point where it is mainly water. Accordingly, a fair proportion of water must be distilled off along with the alcohol, and it so happens that to distil a quantity of water requires much more energy than an equivalent amount of alcohol. A kilo of water requires 2260 kilojoules and a kilo of alcohol requires only 837 kilojoules. Furthermore, as distillation proceeds and more and more water is present in the distillate, the energy costs per litre of the distilled alcohol increases exponentially.

One way to address this would be to minimise the amount of water present in the fermented wash. At present, fermented wash contains about 8% alcohol by volume. This is constrained by the brewing process where sufficient water must be used to allow the wort to drain through the bed of grains. This is basically a technique for separating spent grains from the fermentable material. It has been proved that it is possible to achieve this prior to the addition of any water. By using a suitable mill, the grains are separated dry, and the fermentable material remains as a dry and very fine powder. Whilst it has always been assumed that it is necessary to brew the cereals to produce wort, as in the process for making beer, this has been proved to be unnecessary. It is possible to brew the fine fermentable material at a much lower temperature than the 62.5^0C used in a distillery and as such since it is not necessary to allow for drainage, much less water needs to be added. This results in much higher alcohol content in the wash, which greatly reduces the energy necessary for the first distillation. The only constraint in a process of this type would be that if the final alcoholic content exceeds the level at which yeast can operate, incomplete fermentation will result. If you look at any bottle of red wine, you are likely to see a final alcohol content of 14% indicating that in this case this was the level of alcohol that the yeast was able to tolerate; accordingly, this can be our target in whiskey production.

Pot Still		Column Still	
Wash Strength	Energy Requirement	Wash Strength	Energy Requirement
% Volume	MJ / LPA	% Volume	MJ / LPA
8	13.78	8	4.65
9	12.33	9	4.09
10	11.25	10	3.64
11	10.35	11	3.27
12	9.57	12	2.96
13	8.91	13	2.70
14	8.33	14	2.47

It can be seen from the above that a column still is much more energy efficient than a pot still, and given that much of the energy in a pot still distillation is used once the alcoholic content of the pot is low, there would seem to be a case for starting off the distillation in a pot still taking advantage of both the cooking affect and the other reactions that occur to give the whiskey its character. When the alcoholic content becomes sufficiently low, the liquid can be transferred to a column still to remove the final residue of alcohol and recycle it in the process. It is a small step from here to operate a pot still continuously where all of the important processes such as the cooking take place, and together with other reactions provide taste characteristics and complexity which we associate with pot still.

What we are coming to is a pot column combination where the pot is used to boil up the liquid and generate all the required flavours. This way the pot is fed continuously with wash and at the same time an equal quantity of liquid from the pot is fed to a column where all of the alcoholic fractions, together with the flavour characteristics, are distilled off. The taste of this product can be designed to replicate a standard pot still operation in which the average residence time of the liquid in the pot is designed to be equivalent to the average residence time in the pot still. In the case of the pot still, this value is reckoned to be 50% of the pot still cycle time. It is recognised that when a pot still comes to the boil, spirit is distilled off, which has been exposed to the boiling process for very little time. At the end of the distillation, some of the distillate results from liquid which has been boiled in the pot for the entire cycle time. It is on this basis that the average residence time in a continuous pot still is calculated to be the volume of the liquid in the pot divided by the rate of feed.

In this process the pot still is operated under 100% reflux and all of the distillation is carried in a suitable column. This process can be applied to all of the pot stills: three in the case of the Irish process or two in the Scotch whisky process. As in the description of the wash pot, the same criteria can be used to replicate each stage of the process. This process has been operated at laboratory scale and the assumptions described here have proven to give the desired results.

This process of making whiskey complies in full with the EC definition, although there may be problems describing continuously made pot still as pot still whiskey, or in the case of Scotland, malt whisky. There is very clearly a trade-off between the above process which describes a distillery with zero fossil fuel emissions and the descriptions of the various types of whiskey so produced.

One obvious development would be to operate a combined grain and pot still plant in which the pot plant is operated for three days and the grain plant for a further three days. Grain whiskey is distilled exclusively in columns and as such is much more energy efficient than a pot still plant. Operating this way, the excess methane produced in the grain plant can provide the shortfall in the pot plant.

Chapter 19
Irish Whiskey, The Future

It is now generally accepted that the planet is getting warmer. There is some evidence to back this up, including, unusually heavy rainfall, except in the expected places and severe drought in other places leading to forest fires, other extreme weather includes a greater than usual number of volcanic eruptions and earthquakes. It is also claimed that this has been caused by an increase in the so-called greenhouse gases, mainly carbon dioxide in the atmosphere, caused by burning fossil fuels. If so, it may be possible to halt or even reverse climate change by giving up the use of fossil fuels – coal and oil in its various forms including LPG and natural gas. As distillers we are not qualified to judge on these things, but there are a few facts that cannot be ignored.

- Fossil fuels were created over millions of years and are a finite resource; we are currently using at a much faster rate than they were formed and so they will eventually come to an end, perhaps within one or two centuries.

- Fossil fuels have a number of uses as starting materials for a wide range of different and very useful materials, including such things as plastics, fine chemicals, fertilisers and pharmaceuticals, including lifesaving drugs, and surely it is preferable to prioritise fossil fuels for these purposes rather than actually burning them.

- As the above points are recognised, fossil fuels will become progressively more expensive to burn.

I believe that the human race will not give up on the freedom to have individual transportation vehicles in the future, or to be able to travel by air, both of which currently use oil-based fuels. As far as road vehicles are concerned, there have been some developments in the introduction of electric and hybrid cars, which seem to be quite successful. Hybrid cars use oil-based fuels but use them more efficiently, with such features as regenerative braking. This means that much of the energy used to get the car in motion and up to speed is recovered when the brakes are applied. The electric car depends upon the origin of the electricity used to charge up the battery. There are some new developments in this area including wind and other types of renewable energy. Electricity must be used the instant it is generated and one problem arising from this is the fact that demand is subject to huge peaks and valleys. In general, peak demand comes in the morning and evening and low demand comes overnight. The most efficient way to generate electricity is at a uniform way day and night. Having a large number of electric cars charging overnight will help to smooth out the demand.

In order to continue with individual cars, alcohol can be used as an alternative. Existing oil-based fuels contain no oxygen, and cars and aircraft derive the oxygen required for combustion directly from the atmosphere. Alcohol, on the other hand, does contain oxygen and therefore increases the amount of fuel alcohol to be carried and lowers the miles per gallon or km/litre. Ethanol, that is the alcohol we drink, contains almost 35% oxygen. This weight-increase would render an aircraft very inefficient, but a higher alcohol such as a C^6 or C^8 higher alcohol can reduce the oxygen content to less than 16%, and may provide an alternative fuel for aircraft.

Distilling whiskey, especially in pot stills, is highly energy intensive, energy which currently comes from fossil fuels. If you are a distiller, it might be wise to start to plan for fossil fuel independence as a matter of urgency.

Chapter 20
Conclusion

In this book I have shown the development of whiskeys, particularly Irish whiskey, into an upmarket international product which is regarded as a premium spirit worldwide. In Ireland in particular, essentially all of the raw material is grown on Irish farms and so the final product is almost entirely indigenous (other than casks which are imported), but there is one problem and that is energy.

Distilleries, as outlined in Chapter 18, are energy intensive, deriving their energy from fossil fuels, and as such they make a considerable contribution to the national fossil fuel carbon emissions. Irish whiskey is growing rapidly and provides jobs in farming, malting, distilling, distribution and international marketing, and will play a substantial role in the prosperity of the country. Much of this will be lost unless we adopt an alternative to fossil fuels and their damaging emissions.

Designing a new distillery, or converting an existing one, to operate without the need for fossil fuels has been outlined here and should be a priority. It may require some modifications to traditional processes, but our research shows that if handled properly, successful results can be obtained. Preserving the taste characteristics and quality is a priority and we have proved that this can be achieved. If the above steps are taken, the export of Irish whiskey could make an enormous contribution to the future of the Irish economy.